EAT WITH Intention

Recipes and Meditations for
a Life That Lights You Up

CASSANDRA BODZAK

Creator of *Eat with Intention* TV

Quarto is the authority on a wide range of topics.

Quarto educates, entertains and enriches the lives of our readers—enthusiasts and lovers of hands-on living.

www.quartoknows.com

First published in the United States of America in 2016 by
Race Point Publishing, a member of
Quarto Publishing Group USA Inc.
142 West 36th Street, 4th Floor
New York, NY 10018
www.quartoknows.com

10 9 8 7 6 5 4 3 2 1

ISBN: 978-1-63106-236-0

Library of Congress Cataloging-in-Publication Data

Names: Bodzak, Cassandra, 1987- author.
Title: Eat with intention : recipes and meditations for a life that lights
   you up / Cassandra Bodzak, creator of Eat with Intention TV.
Description: New York : Race Point Publishing, 2016. | Series: Eat with
   intention
Identifiers: LCCN 2016031531 | ISBN 9781631062360 (hardback)
Subjects: LCSH: Self-care, Health--Popular works. | Nutrition--Popular works.
   | Mind and body--Popular works. | BISAC: COOKING / Specific Ingredients /
   Vegetables. | COOKING / Vegetarian & Vegan. | COOKING / Health & Healing /
   Weight Control.
Classification: LCC RA776.95 B63 2016 | DDC 613.2--dc23 LC record available at https://lccn.loc.gov/2016031531

Editorial Director: Jeannine Dillon
Project Editor: Erin Canning
Art Director: Merideth Harte
Photographer: Evi Abeler
Shoot Assistant: Harriet Honkaniemi
Food Stylist: Mariana Velasquez
Assistant Food Stylists: Kristin Stangl and Erika Joyce
Cover and Interior Design: Melissa Gerber

Printed in China

Contents

INTRODUCTION 5

HOW TO USE THIS BOOK: *A Quick Overview* 12

CHAPTER 1: *What Does It Mean to Eat with Intention?* 15

CHAPTER 2: *The Well-Being Trifecta* 35

CHAPTER 3: *Shifting Your Habits* 43

CHAPTER 4: *Taking Care of You* 49

CHAPTER 5: *Integrating Change into Your Daily Life* 55

CHAPTER 6: *Juices and Smoothies* 61

CHAPTER 7: *Breakfast* 81

CHAPTER 8: *Soups* 111

CHAPTER 9: *Salads and Bowls* 131

CHAPTER 10: *Entrées* 153

CHAPTER 11: *Desserts* 177

INDEX 197

ACKNOWLEDGMENTS 204

DEDICATION 205

ABOUT THE AUTHOR 206

DEAR SWEET READER 207

Introduction

I remember once when I was five, my best friend and I were having a play date and we were giggling and chatting on the swings about something that happened at school, but it wasn't long before the subject of weight was raised.

"How much do you weigh?" I asked Ashley. There was a moment of awkward silence between us—a nervous realization that this number might mean something, a mutual worry that one of us might have a "better" number.

After she revealed her weight, we discovered that I weighed more—five pounds more to be exact. I put on my best poker face, and I tried desperately not to cry.

I may have saved face at that moment, but those tears flowed in the years to come. I felt like I lived with this scarlet letter—the F-word—for girls. This badge of not being skinny enough, good enough, or perfect enough lasted well into adulthood. In the third grade, I grabbed my non-existent little tummy while I sat on the toilet, crying to God, "Why did you give me this? Why can't I just be skinny like everyone else?"

I was a normal, healthy weight, but I was so disillusioned with my body at such a young age that, during high school, I clocked hours on the treadmill every morning before class and used weight-loss supplements and pills. One of those mornings, I actually fell asleep while running and face-planted the treadmill. (Talk about your body hitting a wall and refusing to go any further!) There was another early morning when I had just finished my daily treadmill workout complete with a pre-workout diet pill cocktail. As I stood in the shower, my heart started beating like it was coming out of my chest. I thought for sure I was having a heart attack at the ripe old age of 15. In a panic, I tried opening my mouth to drink some of the shower water—hoping that would calm me down—but to my shock, I couldn't even swallow the water. My body was actively expelling whatever I tried to put in it. I crumbled to the shower floor, convinced that this was how my life was going to end. I started to pray.

Dear God, if you let me make it through this, I promise I'll stop with this stupid shit. I promise I won't take the pills anymore. I know they aren't good for me. I'm sorry. I didn't mean it. Give me another chance, and I won't ever do this again.

My pulse slowed, my breath grew deeper, and I felt myself returning to equilibrium. I was going to be okay. I went upstairs and emptied my drawer of diet pills and never spoke a word of the incident to anyone.

My "little" sister Kelsey (left) and me at the Delta Gamma sorority.

My acting girlfriends and me (second from the right) all dressed up for a prom scene on set.

After that, things shifted. My mind was constantly flooded with negative thoughts about my body, but I wasn't willing to jeopardize my health with any more sketchy pills. I may have been self-conscious and unhappy in my skin, but the incident in the shower made me realize that it was more important to be healthy and alive, than to have the body of a Victoria's Secret model. My disordered eating behaviors went dormant for a few more years.

It wasn't until I was at the University of Connecticut getting my BFA in acting that those old, menacing insecurities returned. As you can imagine, it was an extremely competitive environment and there has always been a lot of pressure to be a certain size as an actress. I felt so out of control when it came to auditions. I felt like I couldn't make them like me. I couldn't make them cast me in something. I couldn't make them see that I was worth it. But what I could do was lose weight. If I made myself smaller, I would have a better shot at getting the parts. And once I started getting some parts and established myself, the opportunities would come more easily and I would become a successful actress after college.

I started working out and dieting again. I was going to the gym for a few hours every day and I would eat cereal with skim milk for breakfast, lettuce with fat-free ranch dressing for lunch, and whatever "diet" dinner was available in the dining hall. I was successful in my efforts and I began to lose weight. I started getting compliments, "You lost so much weight! You look great. How are you doing it?" It made me want to keep on going. Suffice to say, I had an unhealthy relationship with my body throughout most of college. A night of partying with pizza and wings meant hating myself and feeling waves of guilt, which I would offset with iceberg lettuce and apples the next day.

This behavior continued until my senior year, when I started to have terrible, debilitating stomach pains—they were like the worst menstrual cramps I'd ever had. I stopped dieting, but that didn't make the pain go away. At the time, I had been taking dance classes—I love dancing—and I had to sit out constantly because the pain was so acute. A couple of weeks later, my teacher Ms. Jean pulled me aside and said, "I don't think this is normal. You need to go to the infirmary and figure out what's going on."

They gave me an assortment of blood tests at the infirmary, and they insisted that I was probably pregnant, which I found both hilarious and offensive. But after all the blood tests over the course of several weeks, the only thing they realized was that I wasn't pregnant. In fact, my tests were clear and they didn't believe there was anything wrong with me. I was released, but I still had the excruciating stomach pains. I knew something wasn't right, but I did not know what to do.

As I made my way out of the building, I ran into an angel (disguised as a nurse). This woman must have seen the exhaustion and frustration on my face and asked me what was going on. After I explained what had just happened, she looked me straight into the eye and asked if I might have

"I knew something wasn't right, but I did not know what to do."

any food allergies. I hadn't, but I was willing to try anything to stop hurting. Something about the way she said it struck a chord in me.

That afternoon, I immersed myself in food allergy research to figure out if this was the answer for me. I figured out that I needed to try an "elimination diet" to help discover what foods might cause a reaction in my body. I was desperate to feel better, so I eliminated a few of the biggies right off the bat: dairy, gluten, and meat. I was definitely a cheeseburger-and-milkshake type of gal when I wasn't restricting, so vegetarianism wasn't something that had ever really crossed my mind.

I bought some vegetables and brown rice, and I made some really basic meals and started eating within my new parameters every day. And that is when the miracle happened. Within three to four days, I felt better. And not just no-more-stomach-cramps-better, but I felt like a completely new human being. I was running on a totally different level of fuel.

To test if you have a food intolerance, you are supposed to start adding the eliminated foods back into your diet to determine which one was causing the pain. I could not even think of reintroducing those foods to my diet, because I enjoyed feeling this good and was terrified the pain would return. I remained on a diet of brown rice and

vegetables for another six months until I began to realize that it wasn't sustainable.

I had to teach myself to cook with a new palette of ingredients; ingredients that didn't include dairy, meat, or gluten. I was starting to miss pizza, brownies, mac and cheese, and chocolate chip cookies! I had loved baking so much and now it felt like I couldn't do that anymore because I had so many restrictions.

I decided to experiment with making vegan brownies. I had never cooked with these sorts of ingredients before, so I was expecting a lot of trial and error. I did some research on common substitutes for eggs and butter as well as naturally gluten-free flour options. And in my tiny little kitchen in my off-campus house, I started making my own vegan baked goods. For me, at this point, I was so excited to have brownies that, of course, they tasted delicious. But I wanted opinions from those who enjoyed regular brownies, so I asked my three roommates. Would they notice my new dairy-free alterations? Would they still enjoy them?

My college roommates, Paige (left), Alex (right), and me (center) at a UCONN football game.

I started putting brownies out for them and not labeling them or telling anyone that they were special. I would just wait until they would be eaten up, and then I would ask the girls for their opinions. Time and time again, they would tell me, "Oh my God, those were amazing!" They were shocked to discover that my brownies were healthier than the "real" thing.

Slowly, more and more friends started asking for my recipes and wanting to know what new foods I was making. Before long they talked me into creating a website where I could keep all my recipes for them to see whenever they wanted to. And that was the birth of the blog.

When it began, it was called *Cassie's Confections*, and it was mostly just my healthy baked goods. It was a basic WordPress site with one of the preprogrammed free themes, and I slapped up a black-and-white photo of cupcakes for the header. It wasn't anything to look at and it, just something for me to share my little concoctions with friends.

It was only after I graduated that it became something that I would look forward to doing. It became a creative hobby for me while I faced the reality of multiple unsatisfying part-time jobs during my first year in the city. I always enjoyed cooking. Every so often I would go in the kitchen and whip up something new, and then I would hop on the blog and post about it. And it really just sat there trucking along as a passion project for years while I was acting and working on other jobs in the city to stay afloat. It never felt like work because I loved to do it. I certainly never set out for it to be anything more than that.

When I finally started to reintroduce some of those suspected food culprits in my life, I figured out instantly which foods were the problems. My first attempt at chicken almost landed me in the emergency room because the pain was so acute.

Similarly with dairy, I would also have stomach pains, although they were much milder than the pains I had when eating meat. If I ate a significant amount of dairy, I would break out in hives, and it would feel as though a ball of hair was lodged in my throat. Gluten was the mildest of all for me, only causing some brain fog and mild acne breakouts. I could still consume it without much pain, but I mentally noted that it wasn't necessarily working wonders for my body. I removed many things from my diet at once, which might not have been the best idea, but I felt dramatically better almost immediately. My energy soared and my intense stomach pains vanished. I was absolutely addicted to how good it felt, and I never wanted to go back to that pain again.

KENNY AND PSC

Things were going well with what I lovingly called "my kitchen therapy" until May 4, 2013. I was living in Astoria, Queens, at the time and was walking home when my mom called with the kind of news that freezes time and changes your entire outlook on life. She told me that my little brother, Kenny—who was twenty-three at the time—had an autoimmune disease called *primary sclerosing cholangitis* (PSC) paired with *ulcerative colitis*. I had never heard of this before, but with each word she spoke, I felt like I was crumbling little by little with each step back to my apartment.

PSC is a rare disease that causes inflammation and impedes the flow of bile from the liver to intestines, which will cause liver failure and possibly liver and bile duct cancer. It is often paired with ulcerative colitis, as in Kenny's case, which causes inflammation and ulcers in the intestines. It's extremely painful and debilitating. While medication can be used to keep symptoms and pain at bay, there is no cure other than a liver transplant.

The second I got home, I made the mistake of looking up the disease online, including prognosis and life expectancy. Then I fell to pieces in the corner of my living room. *How could I go about life knowing that my brother's could be ending?* By early morning, I dragged myself out of the corner and crawled to the shower, where I curled up in the fetal position. I sobbed as the warm water hit my back. How could I be strong, knowing what Kenny had to go through? It was on that bathroom floor—desperate for comfort or relief, I'm not sure which—that in my deep surrender I started talking to God, the universe, or whoever was still awake in Astoria and could hear my cries: *I don't know what to do. Can't you let me have this disease instead of him? He's too young and doesn't deserve to die. How am I supposed to handle this? How can I keep living? I can't. Please tell me how to do this.*

Kenny and me wearing our token matching Christmas sweaters.

"How could I go about life knowing that my brother's could be ending?"

A symphony of *"please tell me what to do"* and *"help me"* continued for what must have been over an hour. I pleaded and bargained with whatever higher power was listening until a blanket of calm came over my entire body. It was as if a parent had found me lying there shaking in the tub, and placed a warm towel over me. I heard a voice inside say, *Go to bed, my child. Tonight, just go to bed.* I slinked off to bed and passed out

almost instantly, my body exhausted from hours of sobbing.

When I woke up the next morning, I immediately felt the need to meditate and began researching it online. I didn't have the time or luxury to go off to India to study at an ashram nor could I afford to pay someone a thousand dollars to whisper a mantra in my ear. I needed help pronto. So there I was, spending day after day in bed, trying every meditation offered on YouTube.

Those messy, imperfect, exploratory days kicked off my daily spiritual practice and opened me up to a whole new world. I was ready to learn more, and all the meditation I was doing had nourished me in a way I couldn't describe. I found books such as *Spirit Junkie* by Gabby Bernstein, *A Return to Love* by Marianne Williamson, and *A Course in Miracles*. Once I became open and ready to receive guidance, it was like the universe was pushing the books off the shelves and making sure the right videos caught my eye. I grew more interested in spirituality and began meditating several times a day so that I could be a support system for my brother and my family. As a result of my new life support system, my food blog suddenly became this beautiful, creative outlet for me and had this whole new spiritual life that I was beginning to weave into it.

Baking and cooking healthy and delicious foods became my support system—and in so many ways—my therapy—during those months. It was my meditation before I knew to meditate, and it's still a very sacred process to me even to this day. I was posting on the blog more than ever because it made me feel good and—naturally, with time and love—it flourished. One day, I decide it would be fun to make a few cooking videos for YouTube, so I filmed them using my laptop, which sat on a stack of cookbooks on a kitchen stool. I remember adjusting the camera angle so that I could film it all in one take without ever changing camera position. It was a hilarious hot mess, but I had so much fun with it. At the time, I gave myself permission to do whatever it took to make myself happy.

And then on one unsuspecting Friday afternoon, I received a call from someone at ABC who asked me to audition for a new show with Anthony Bourdain, Nigella Lawson, Ludo Lefebvre, and Marcus Samuelsson called *The Taste*. I remember thinking they must have made a mistake and called the wrong person. I even asked the woman, "How did you find me? Are you sure you know what kind of cooking I do? I don't think any of these people are fans of my healthy vegan cooking." They were sure, though. I didn't know if this would be my path, but that little voice inside told me I had to do it. And so I did the show. With one giant leap of faith and a few batches of gluten-free vegan cupcakes later, my life was transformed forever.

It all sunk in while I was filming on the Universal Studios lot. Being on the show and surrounded by professional chefs helped me figure out who I was. All my experiences—the pain, the food allergies, and my brother's terminal illness—I needed to experience them so that I could help others get through them, too. I needed to find my journey back to joy so others could find their joy, too. I

believe I was placed on this path for a reason. My mission was to show people how to tap into the power of food, meditation, and self-care so they could transform and elevate their lives. They could live their bliss despite whatever personal traumas might happen along the way. And they do happen to all of us, at some point or another. Loving yourself can make you an unstoppable force of good in the world, even in the face of pain and suffering.

A LIFE THAT LIGHTS YOU UP

Eat with Intention is something that I feel was birthed straight out of my soul. I remember doing a 31-minute Kundalini meditation (*Long Ek Ong Kars*) in my New York apartment and asking for guidance for what to do next in my life. At the time, I had been coaching people one-on-one, developing recipes and videos, and I was enjoying all the opportunities that were floating to my plate. I knew I was ready for a bigger task, the next step.

So I did this beautiful meditation and at the end of it, I felt this waterfall gushing through me, as I frantically wrote down the idea for *Eat with Intention*, which—at its core—is merging food, meditation, and self-care. Teaching them all as one, instead of the separation we so often see in the media, cooking shows, and other cookbooks or lifestyle programs. Food, meditation, and self-care can help create a foundation that will support our most joyful lives on this planet. Each one is sacred and powerful on its own, but together they are unstoppable.

Food is one of those things that you can't escape. It's a necessity that can either work for you or against you, but you have to decide if you want to take that relationship you have with food and your body to a more loving level. People often don't even make it to the self-awareness stage if they are still trapped in the conversation around food and their body. Meditation and self-care are potent tools that can really harness and elevate these powerful instruments that our minds and bodies are. It was only in breaking free from my disordered behavior around food and embracing my body that I was able to go deeper and cultivate the fruits of my self-care and, later, my mediation practice.

Through this first doorway of food, you will embark on a holistic journey of well-being and begin a life where feeling good isn't an occasional occurrence, but an everyday gift. It is possible to eat amazing food that is healthy, makes you feel good, and puts you into a different energetic state, but the reality is that the food conversation is just the beginning. It's an entry point to a conversation that involves utilizing your mind, body, and soul to live your greatest life on Earth. It's not just about delicious recipes, vegan brownies, eating kale all the time, and drinking green smoothies. It's about the intention behind it and your relationship with food. It's about the why. *Why are you eating this way?* I spent many years eating kale and lettuce from a really unhealthy place. I truly believe it would have been better for me to be eating French fries from a really loving place than eating the kale from a place of guilt and self-loathing. In fact, let me say this now: I don't care if you use the recipes in this book. I hope they simply get you in the kitchen and in the joy of nourishing yourself. It's about shifting the conversation you have every single day with your body; it's about getting you into a loving and nurturing relationship with your body; and it's about creating rituals in your life by incorporating meditation and simple self-care exercises so that you can be fully supported in living your best life with a clear head, open heart, and bounds of energy.

We are all at different points in our food-life journey, and I wish I had this book as a guide when

I first started out. I think that is why I am beyond excited to share this sacred manual with you. Life is too short to feel badly about your body or hate yourself for what you eat. I look forward to walking beside you on your journey to eating with intention and showing you the blueprint to designing a life that lights you up from the inside out.

— Cassandra Bodzak

How to Use This Book: A Quick Overview

This is not your traditional cookbook. This book is about giving you the tools to get in the kitchen and experience the joy of nourishing yourself; it's about shifting the conversation you have every single day with your body; it's about getting you into a loving and nurturing relationship with your body; and it's about creating rituals in your life by incorporating meditation and simple self-care exercises so that you can be fully supported in living your best life with a clear head, open heart, and bounds of energy.

RECIPES

The recipes in this book have been designed to engage you in a mindful experience with what's on your plate. Each recipe has its own assigned mantra (e.g., "My beauty radiates from within." "I honor my basic needs." "I choose to do things I love."), which is purposefully paired with a specific meditation or mindfulness exercise. For easy reference, the opening page of each cooking chapter lists the mantras followed by the recipe names. You may use them in any way you want, but I've made a few suggestions here.

- Choose a recipe from this book that appeals to you, prepare the dish, and then read the meditation. Ponder it. Entertain the idea that perhaps being drawn to that specific recipe was indeed a way to bring you to that message. You can read the meditation in the morning before you start cooking or in the evening after you've finished.

- If you are seeking inspiration from a message, let's say to "be open to unexpected opportunities," then turn to the recipe that holds that intention (in this case, page 175) and utilize the corresponding meditation and mantra to create a ritual to put forth that intention and enjoy its accompanying recipe.

- Use the book like a tarot deck or oracle (my favorite!). Close your eyes with the book in hand and ask for guidance. Then open your book randomly to a page and receive whatever message and meal is waiting for you.

Though I don't endorse a specific diet, I do believe as a whole we can all benefit tremendously by incorporating more plant-based meals into our diets. I'm passionate about sharing these kind of recipes, and all of the recipes in this book are vegan. I also am a huge proponent of buying organic. My mission is to simply get you eating more of the good stuff!

MEDITATION 101

I am a big advocate of a daily meditation/ mindfulness practice, which I talk about in much more detail starting on page 37. Even if it's just for one minute a day, start where you are comfortable, but don't be afraid to turn up your practice to correspond with your current needs. You might even be in a regular gratitude or meditation practice already, but if you want to improve the relationship with your body and end the war with it, then you need to express gratitude for all that your body does for you every single day. After all, when you love your body unconditionally, it's usually from a place of tremendous gratitude for it.

Here are some basic explanations of a few meditation terms that you may see throughout this book.

Kundalini: This is the school of yoga that I practice and am a certified instructor of. Many of the meditations in this book follow the Kundalini tradition.

Easy pose: All Kundalini meditations begin by sitting cross-legged in easy pose with a straight spine. I'm sitting in easy pose with my hands in gyan mudra (see below for *mudra*) in the photo to the right!

Mudra: This is the position and placement of your hands while meditating. A lot of the exercises in the book don't specify a mudra so you can have your hands in a relaxed, comfortable position. The ones that do specify a mudra include an illustration, like the to the right (especially if the mudra is not self-explanatory in the instructions).

All Kundalini meditations begin with "easy pose."

CHAPTER 1

What Does It Mean to Eat with Intention?

Have you ever made cupcakes and accidentally screwed up the batter? Maybe you used an incorrect amount of flour or baking powder, and your cake turned out a bit wonky. Instead of throwing out the batter and starting all over, you made the most incredible frosting and slathered it on top. *Voilà!* Though you managed to disguise the problem, you didn't actually fix the cake.

Well, every time you try the latest diet craze—whether it's low-carb, paleo, sugar-free, or whatever—you're hiding the cake. It's why you constantly feel frustrated when it comes to your body and the food you are putting in it. It's why dieting is always so hard and feels like a chore. Often, after you successfully lose a few pounds, it eventually slides back on plus some. In this book, I will show you how to make peace with your body, heal your relationship with food, and eat with intention. I will help you fix the cake.

In many ways, I was very lucky for things to go the way they did for me. Getting sick in college, with those debilitating stomach pains and feeling my body struggle shook me awake earlier than most. It was only after going through all that pain, all those blood tests, and doctor visits, and no solid diagnosis from anyone in the medical field, that I really woke up to what I was putting into my body and how poorly I had been taking care of myself. I had been looking at my body as the enemy for most of my life. My body was this "thing" I was stuck with, and I was constantly

wanting it to be smaller here, curvier there, more toned here, and so on. I didn't appreciate then that I had been given this body as a gift; instead, I spent years resenting my figure because it wasn't my so-called ideal!

Once I became genuinely concerned for my well-being, that changed entirely. After no doctor could tell me what was wrong with me, and why I was in so much pain all the time, I decided to see if I could help myself. I eliminated all the foods that I thought might be harmful to my body, and my life completely changed in just a matter of days. It still brings tears to my eyes remembering those first days of feeling like a new human and recognizing how good my body could actually feel. Once I got a taste of the energy I was truly capable of having, I never wanted to mistreat my body again—I was hooked. I felt like my body and I were on the same team for the first time since I was five. I totally released the desire to be a certain size or shape and solely wanted it to be healthy, to be functional, and to feel good.

Eating with intention is the deceptively simple

ishment, how much rest it needs, and how much to move and sweat—is far more valuable. *Your* body knows what it needs better than anyone else, including me. Our bodies are highly intelligent, and we need to respect and honor that wisdom. So how do you begin eating with intention?

After reflecting on my own experience around food and love, I realized there are four main pillars of the journey. I use the term "pillars," and not steps, because this isn't necessarily a linear process. You may find one pillar a more comfortable place to start than another, so be sure to honor what you need at this moment. And even when you feel like you have mastered all four pillars, a bad habit could rear its ugly head again a few years down the road. Like the time you baked cookies for a friend's event and then proceeded to eat **every single one** while they were still warm from the oven, not only giving yourself a violent stomachache, but also leaving you with no choice but to show up with a store-bought dessert instead. Think of these four pillars as your toolbox, and you should use them to bring yourself back to your truth. Learn them now to transform your relationship with your body, but also keep them in a safe place just in case any loose screws need a little tightening down the road.

PILLAR 1: MAKING PEACE WITH YOUR BODY

So how can you shift your relationship with your body *without* having to go through some illness or medical drama? While you might not be experiencing acute pain, I would guess that most of you are tired of feeling sluggish, tired of feeling bloated, and tired of being unhappy with the status quo. Most of us are practically programmed to fight against our body. That's why detoxes, cleanses, diet pills, crazy exercise routines, and fat-removing surgeries are growing more popular in our culture. When we think of our body as an opponent, we have a conditional level of love for

name for a process that involves shifting the relationship between food and your body. It means eating from a place of self-love and awareness. And I don't mean that fake, pretend self-love you see all over social media dressed up as bright pink quotes and selfies with flowers; I'm talking about that deep, soulful self-love that comes when you genuinely heal the relationship with your body and connect to your soul. I wish it were as simple as throwing a pretty, peppy, inspirational affirmation over your food before you eat and pretending everything is all better, but let's be real. If it were that easy, we all would have done that during puberty when most of us first starting waging war with our bodies.

In this book, I will share my thoughts on the types of nourishment our bodies crave as well as delicious recipes to help us satisfy those cravings. However, learning the process of making peace with yourself, healing the unhealthy patterns you have around food, and listening to your body—so that it can tell you what it actually needs for nourit: "I will love my body *after* this juice cleanse, because I will be less bloated and lose that excess weight." or "I will love my body *after* this 90-day cardio-and-ab challenge because I'll finally have a defined stomach." Our love for our bodies is always placed at some later date after it's bended to our desires of what it should look like or weigh.

Now, what if you shifted to thinking of your body like your partner's body? Maybe your boyfriend or husband's body isn't perfect. Maybe he could be a little more toned around his stomach or lose a few pounds, but I bet you would never make that a condition of your love for him. In fact, most of us know that when we love from that unconditional place, we actually give people the freedom to become the best version of themselves on their own accord. Unconditional love has the power to transform.

> "We actually give people the freedom to become the best version of themselves."

This was one of those tools I picked up way down the line. I had been years into my journey of having a more loving relationship with my body when I spent a few weeks traveling in Barcelona and Paris. I was far from my normal eating habits and workout routine and just allowing myself to enjoy all the fresh, local food that my travels had to offer, when I noticed my clothes fitting a little tighter than usual, my face was looking puffy, and that all-too-familiar feeling of being uncomfortable

in my body came up again. One evening in Paris, after really going to town on a fresh baguette and some Brie, I had an extreme allergic reaction. My breathing became shallow, my chest broke out in hives, and my throat felt like it had a large ball of hair in it. I panicked. I was alone in a foreign country, and I didn't want to go to a hospital by myself. I decided to remain calm. I turned on a nice hot shower and calmed my breathing. I drank a ton of water, crawled into bed, and I fell asleep. When I woke up the next morning, many of the symptoms disappeared but I was angry and disgusted with myself: *You know you can't eat dairy. You know bread bothers your stomach. Why did you do that? You are so weak. You need to do a juice cleanse for the rest of the trip and run along the Seine every day so you won't be so gross when you get back home.*

HOLD UP!

I thought those days were behind me. I hadn't been that mean to myself in years, and I had to break the cycle of negative thoughts. Yes, I did

feel incredibly uncomfortable in my body. Yes, I did wish that I hadn't ventured into bread-and-Brie land. But luckily, I had my toolbox, and I knew that making my body the enemy was not the answer. At that moment, I knew that I needed to treat my body like I would treat a loved one. I needed to love it regardless of whether it was five pounds up or down. I needed to love it and let my pure love give it the safety to be exactly as it wanted to be. I was ready for an even deeper level of peace with my physical being, and once again, it took a bit of scare to shake me up into it.

So despite feeling the draw of a 3-day juice cleanse to right my wrongs, I decided to make peace with my body and not punish it. I sat there on the bed of the small apartment I was renting, I put a hand on my heart and a hand on my belly, and I cried. I apologized to my body and apologized to myself. I thanked my body for being strong, and I asked what it needed to feel better. And I knew that the answer wasn't to spend the rest of my trip living on liquid and running laps. My body wanted me to live, it wanted me to soak up all Paris had to offer; it simply wanted less bread and more greens, and a home-cooked meal or two if I could manage it. Eating out for several weeks was taking its toll on my system.

I listened, and within a few days, I started feeling more like myself. My bloating vanished and eventually the few extra pounds shed its own. Paris is the city of love, and it's impossible to deny it. That trip shifted the relationship I had with my body to an even deeper loving place than it had been before.

Gratitude

The other major component of having a peaceful, loving relationship with your body, your temple, is gratitude. Some people might be used to expressing gratitude for different aspects of their lives like friends, family, nature, or spirituality. You might even be in a regular gratitude practice or meditation already, but if you want to improve the relationship with your body and end the war with it, then you need to express gratitude for all that your body does for you every single day. After all, when you love your body unconditionally, it's usually from a place of tremendous gratitude for it. I experienced my first step of gratitude back in college when I started eliminating the foods that were hurting my body, and I finally had the energy and wellness to go about my day again. However, it was when I heard about and began to understand my younger brother's illness that my appreciation for my body deepened to a level I could not have imagined.

> "Growing up, he was the kind of kid that I always saw as invincible."

Kenny had always been a tall, handsome, strong guy with a brilliant mind and a bit of a dark sense of humor. He started working out pretty young and would love to walk around the house shirtless when we were in high school, eating a full gallon of mint-chocolate-chip ice cream and teasing me with his washboard abs. Growing up, he was the kind of kid that I always saw as invincible, unlike myself. I remember when I first found out what was going on inside his body, I couldn't stop picturing his intestines being ravaged from the inside out, his basic bodily functions failing, and his entire body wasting away in the process from all the incredibly toxic "medicine" his doctors were feeding him just to keep him alive. All I wanted to do was trade bodies. I wanted to give him my intestines, my liver, whatever he needed. It all felt so unfair. Watching him made me realize how much I had

*Ah, siblings . . . It might look like we're hugging at first, but
I'm actually trying to get Kenny in a chokehold here.*

taken my body for granted. I just *expected* it to work, and it did without a single acknowledgment from me about how truly amazing that is.

"Watching him made me realize how much I had taken my own body for granted."

Spending those months in and out of hospitals with my brother changed everything for me. As I watched him get treatment after treatment, become as frail as a skeleton, and eventually lose his large intestine and get a colostomy bag for his small intestine just to excrete waste, I actually started getting emotional every time I went to the bathroom. You never stop to think what an incredible privilege it is to have a fully functioning digestive system that absorbs the nutrients in your food and then eliminates everything else in a regular, pain-free process. I had been putting crazy diet pills and overly processed "fat-free" chemical-laden food into my body for so many years that I felt so lucky my body was still trucking along in good condition. I was grateful deep down to my cells.

I used to think I was one of the unfortunate few who has to watch a loved one suffer the way my brother does, but after years of speaking engagements and classes, I've realized the unfortunate truth that far too many of you can relate to my story and also have a relative or loved one—whether they are alive or have passed away—that has impacted the way you feel about your own working body. I discovered that a body gratitude

meditation practice is a great way to become really present and connected to this deep cellular level of gratitude.

Take a few moments in the shower each morning to do an inventory of your body and say thank you for everything that you can. I'd say thank you for my beautiful legs that are strong and allow me to do yoga and walk all over the city with ease. Thank you for my stomach and intestines that allow me to process all the food I eat and give me loving nudges when I'm eating something that my body doesn't like. Thank you for my arms that carry my groceries and hug my loved ones. Thank you for my heart that beats every single day and centers me when I get too caught up in my thoughts. Thank you for lungs that allow me to take for granted my breath most moments of the day and fill me with such beautiful air and life. Thank you for my nose that allows me to smell the flowers and freshly baked cookies. Thank you to my ears that let me listen to my favorite music and hear the sweet voices of those I love. You get the idea.

Be specific, be sincere, and choose things that feel authentic. Start off small if you find the exercise hard. So even if you don't like the size of your nose, perhaps you can express gratitude for the wonderful things it allowed you to smell today. When I first began doing this gratitude ritual, I knew it wasn't fancy and some days I would skip parts, but I would always spend just a few minutes connecting with my physical being. I still do this every morning in the shower. It grounds me back in my commitment to having a peaceful partnership with my body and puts me in a state of deep love and respect for it. If you want further inspiration, I've recorded an even more detailed guided meditation for deep body gratitude that you can listen to at **www.cassandrabodzak.com/ eatwithintention**. Spending a few minutes each day bowing to the miracles that naturally occur inside of you is essential to improving the relationship with your body, and I can't recommend it enough.

End Negative Self-Talk

The hardest part of making peace with your body is quieting that menacing negative self-talk. You know the kind I mean. The voice that tells you your thighs are too big. Or the one that calls you a pig after having pizza with your friends. While having a deep sense of love and appreciation for your body will lower the volume on that mean voice inside that never feels you're good enough, you still need to actively stop yourself every single time you think or say something negative about your body. That voice is not the real you. In Michael Singer's *The Untethered Soul*, he compares this voice to a very rude roommate, and I love that analogy. If thinking of that voice as a rude roommate makes you laugh, even better. It will have less power over you.

Through your daily gratitude practice, you will gain some altitude in the situation, meaning you will be able to look at it from above instead of from inside, and the view is always clearer from above.

"*By laughing at those negative thought patterns you disarm them . . .*"

Stopping Negative Thought Patterns

1. Pause. Take a few deep breaths.

2. Bring in your gratitude.

3. If you are struggling with Step 2, acknowledge that your nasty roommate is holding the mic right now. Acknowledgment is a powerful tool on its own.

Laughter is Spiritual

If you feel tempted to judge yourself in a harsh or negative way, I urge you to remedy it with a nice big laugh at yourself. Laughing has become a deep spiritual practice for me. It instantly shifts the energy away from my inner critic and into a space of joy and deep love for myself. For instance, last winter, I started getting my favorite Brazil nut chai from Peacefood Café in Union Square and began ordering it alongside one of their big, delicious, vegan, and gluten-free chocolate chip cookies. It developed into a daily ritual, and I remember thinking to myself, *You are so hooked on this cookie-chai combo, Cass! Tsk, tsk.* But instead of judging myself harshly, I started laughing at myself while walking down the street as I chomped down on the cookie. Instead of judging myself for the behavior, the laughter helped me look at myself (and the situation) from above. I even liken it to seeing myself as a child: it was funny and cute that I was so hooked on these enormous chocolate chip cookies and chai. This might sound a little out there if you haven't given it a try, but I highly recommend faking it until you make it with this one. It's helped me shift those negative thought patterns by leaps and bounds.

The beautiful thing about the laughter is that I still acknowledged the situation, I saw the pattern, I held myself with love, and I didn't make it such a serious issue, so I was able to shift my behavior effortlessly. How did I do it? I started frequenting a tea place instead, so those giant cookies didn't tempt me. The important thing here is that I did it out of love, because I knew I didn't want my body to be on autopilot with my need for a daily sugar fix.

This laughing technique is also a great weapon when it comes to negative self-talk. Let's say you are trying on that less-than-flattering bridesmaid's dress (surprise, surprise) that your friend picked out for you. As you look in the mirror, you suddenly hear that little voice start shouting, "If you lost five pounds, you would actually be able to zip this thing!" Before you continue down that path of self-abuse, hear it and try to see the situation from above—you are in the dressing room wearing a hideous dress and that annoying voice is telling you to lose weight! Take a moment to laugh at yourself and the absurdity of the situation! By laughing at those negative thought patterns, you disarm them, and they won't have the same power over you. So laugh your beautiful face off, my dear!

If you are not quite in the space for laughter yet around your negative self-talk, it's okay. I've been there too. The first step to navigating those mean thoughts is to realize that they are not your truth; that's why Singer's "rude roommate" analogy is so good. Let's separate the real you, which is pure love, from the crazy voice in your head that's out to make you feel unworthy. Once you recognize those thoughts as separate from your core self, you can begin to disarm them. Your daily gratitude practice

is your first line of defense here because you cannot be in fear and gratitude at the same time, meaning you can't appreciate your gorgeous body that allows you to laugh and go shopping with your girl-friends while simultaneously condemning it for not being able to squeeze into that too-tight brides-maid's dress. You are either in gratitude or not, so if you try to separate yourself from the negative thought when it arrives, recognize it as fear (even call it fear), and then you can return to a space of love by getting present with gratitude again.

I want to be clear here: old thought patterns die hard and this is a mindful muscle that you build over time by being in the situation and muscling your way through the process until it starts coming more naturally. I also know that, sometimes, you want to break down in tears in the dressing room because that dress doesn't fit, and it just feels terrible. Trust me, I've been there. In those times, treat yourself as you would a best friend and care for yourself so that you don't spiral further down. If you start to see yourself spi-raling into a negative thought pattern, here's what you should do first.

An old Cherokee parable tells the story of the two wolves. In every man, there are two wolves fighting: one is a good wolf and one is a bad wolf. The one who wins inside is the one you feed. You need to starve that "bad wolf," or your negative thought patterns, by removing that power over your decision-making. Don't skip dinner that night or go running because that dress didn't fit. Don't eat everything in your kitchen because the dress didn't fit either. Feed the good wolf. Enjoy the rest of the night with your friends and eat a normal meal like you intended.

You may not always be able to silence your neg-ative self-talk, but you can certainly nip it in the bud before it bleeds into more destructive behaviors.

PILLAR 2: BECOMING A FOOD DETECTIVE

My journey away from the foods that worked against me to food that made me feel good was abrupt and dramatic, like ripping off a Band-Aid. It's a good approach if you are in a lot of pain or struggling with a particular illness, but there is also a gentler and more gradual way to go about the same process. After years of working with clients who wanted to find out what foods were energizing them and what foods weren't working with their body, I've lovingly dubbed this practice "becoming a food detective."

Start a Food-Mood Journal

The first step involves bringing more awareness to *what* you are eating and *why* you are eating it. Start by keeping a food-mood journal. Many diets recommend regularly logging what you eat, and I am recommending this too, but the food-mood journal is not about restriction or counting calo-

ries. Spending a few days becoming more aware of your food can be a pretty big wake-up call. I have seen people in the first few days of this process realize almost immediately that they get a "dairy stomachache" after their usual breakfast of a bacon-egg-and-cheese sandwich. Others reach for coffee and a donut in the mid-afternoon to wake up, but the sugar-caffeine jolt ends up making them feel worse. When you start journaling, the answers will be right in front of you—you're just finally making yourself more aware of the patterns.

The most important part of this pillar is that it is a JUDGMENT-FREE zone. I'm serious about this! Gathering this information is *not* meant to give more ammunition to that negative voice in your head. This is just data collection, so I beg you to look with compassion. It's also the perfect time to remind you that we *all* have weird behaviors around food: places we go to on autopilot without thinking about them, or certain repeat indulgences. You are human, I am human, and I don't know if I could even trust a person who has never been tempted by some leftover cookie dough in the fridge or binged on a heaping plate of fries!

Now we're ready to get down and dirty with the detective work here. Your food-mood journal can be any journal. You can jot down notes on your smartphone, download an app, or simply use a nice notebook that you can carry with you throughout the day.

The 2-Week Food-Mood Challenge

The real trick to this exercise is to NOT be on your best behavior around food for those 2 weeks. I don't suggest you behave like a starving college student at an all-you-can-eat buffet, but to be normal and allow your regular habits to come through. You don't want to shift into hyper-clean eating for 2 weeks while you keep a log of your food and mood, and then go right back to how you *actually* eat afterward, because you wouldn't get a good read of your real day-to-day habits. So please just be honest.

Log Challenge!

Up for a challenge? For the next 2 weeks, after you complete your food-mood detective work, check in with your body before and after every meal. Before you decide what to put in your body, simply ask what it wants. We don't realize how we operate on autopilot around our food choices, even healthy ones. We get into a routine around what we eat for breakfast or the item we always have for lunch, and we don't check in with ourselves. One of our body's deepest needs is variety. It craves different foods because it needs all kinds of vitamins, minerals, and nutrients. So when we become robots around our food choices, we deprive our body of this core desire. Remember, we are doing reps and building our intention muscles here, so really go for it: ask your body for more guidance than feels comfortable, really push yourself, and try this new way of operating on for size. Ask about everything. If you are feeling tired or unfocused, ask about that too.

• Log *all* of your meals, snacks, and beverages! Yes, even that handful of M&M's at 3:30 p.m. during the staff meeting and the half of a gin and tonic you had during happy hour—everything! Don't cheat yourself here. The more honest you are, the clearer the picture will be of your regular diet. Also be sure to include things that you add to your foods like milk in your coffee or Sriracha® on your eggs.

• Log how you feel before you eat the meal as well as how you feel 30 minutes to an hour post-meal. For example, if you're feeling stressed when you head out to lunch, log it! And if you decide to eat a grilled cheese sandwich with tomato soup and then an hour later you are falling asleep at your desk, note it all! And again, no judgment here. We are just collecting valuable clues for your own mind-body-food case.

• Log your focus and energy level throughout the day. Now you don't need to be super intense with this; it's good enough just to note the big arcs, every 4 hours or so. This helps you see when in the day you are energized and when you are tired.

After the initial 2-week period, some of my clients also find it helpful to bring their food-mood journals back in a few weeks' time if they notice a sudden dip in energy or mood, bloating, or any other uncomfortable symptom. Some will also bring it when they go away on a trip because it helps them see what foods are working for them as they introduce different meals, remove certain ingredients, and incorporate different activities into their life.

The Results Are In!

After your initial 2 weeks, sit down with your log and a few colored highlighters. I would start by highlighting all the times you felt extremely exhausted with one color, and then go back and see if there are any similarities in the foods you ate on those days. I bet you are going to be floored at how apparent some of the connections are right off the bat. Perhaps you notice that every time you eat a sandwich for lunch, you can barely keep your eyes open after 2 p.m., but on the days you eat a salad, it's not nearly as intense and you make it till about 5 p.m. before getting a bit sluggish or vice versa. Take a different color highlighter and note all the instances you felt sick or had a stomachache. Look for patterns. Did you have a common food like dairy or gluten before all your stomach issues? It's important that during this process you focus on just a few BIG things that really make a significant impact on your energy or well-being and not overwhelm yourself by trying to find every single thing in your diet or lifestyle habits that may be causing you some discomfort.

When I go over the food-mood logs of the participants in my Eat with Intention online program, I can usually laser in on the top three major issues and deduce the possible culprits through the patterns I see in behavior, mood, and ingredients. Is it possible you have ten different foods that are not working for your body? Absolutely, but take care of the big problem foods first. If your leg is broken, you probably want to get that taken care of first before you handle the minor cuts and bruises on your arms! Pay attention to your body. Any time you experience any physical pain or a total lack of energy or focus, then that is probably the place you will experience the greatest transformation by making some simple swaps in your diet or routine.

Take action on only one or two educated associations that you can see from your log. For example, you might decide to remove dairy from your diet and see if that eliminates any stomachaches you were experiencing. That one adjustment is absolutely plenty to start. If I also noticed that I regularly feel bloated and exhausted after I eat, then I could also potentially try to be more conscious about slowing down and properly chewing my food completely during meals. Whatever you deduce, make sure you commit to the elimination or change for the next three weeks and notice what happens. Did the stomachaches vanish as soon as the dairy did? How were your energy levels once you started making slower eating and intentional chewing a regular occurrence?

We all have different reactions to the foods or behaviors that aren't working for our body, so it's important to honor the observations in your diet and to get into the habit of communicating with your body, which brings me to the third pillar—starting a conversation.

PILLAR 3: STARTING A CONVERSATION

When was the last time you really sat down, tuned in, and had a heart-to-heart with your body? It might sound odd to "meet and go over everything," but talking to your body can be a transformative experience. Our body is brilliant and knows exactly what it needs to run at its best. We will often dismiss its cries for help so that feeling bad actually starts to feel normal.

There has been a lot of speculation about how we choose the food we eat, and it has been suggested that when you walk around the farmers' market, you are actually more visually attracted to fruits and vegetables that contain the vitamins and nutrients your body needs at that moment. Given our foraging ancestors, that would make perfect sense. They would need to find nutrient-rich food to survive. I could never figure out why I never wanted to put tomatoes or peppers into anything I cooked until I was tested for several different food allergies. I discovered that tomatoes and peppers were inflammatory for my body, so it made perfect sense that I never wanted to cook with them. I listen to my body now, and I trust what it's trying to tell me. We just need to filter out the noise of the media and food industry that color what we "think" we need.

The First Steps

Let's start at the beginning. How can you start a conversation with your body if you have never tried to consciously communicate with it? The answer is simple. All it takes is a willingness to listen and creating the space to hear what it has to say. Try the meditation below to start opening up the channels of communication:

Close your eyes, place your hands on your heart, and take a few long, deep breaths. Release any tension, stress, or strain that you have and allow any thoughts to pass by like clouds. Let them float along, bring yourself back to your breath, back in your body. Now ask your body silently, how have I been treating you? What do you need to feel your best? How I can take better care of you? Allow silence after each question to give you the space to hear the answers. Keep a notebook nearby if you feel the need to write anything down. Honor whatever it is you hear.

This might feel awkward at first and you may not know what to make of it, but that's perfectly fine. We are building a lifelong partnership here, and it will take time before you pick up on the subtleties. The most important thing is that you are making the time to ask the questions and allowing for the space to hear the answers. As you get better at listening to your body, this "check in" process can be even more casual. It can even be a deep breath in and an honest question. Keep it simple so you can do it anywhere, even if you are out to eat or in the supermarket shopping for the week. The point is to be in an ongoing dialogue with your body so that you know what it needs and how best to take care of it.

Developing this habit will save you from the more painful ways your body will try to communicate with you. When your body isn't being heard, that's when we tend to get sick. Our body cries out for help in all sorts of ways: infections, tumors, digestive issues, skin conditions, and even cancer. If you are at that point, then I am so glad that you have found this book along your journey. If you are not in that position, you can learn through ease and joy and discover the wisdom rooted deep in your cells right now before any ailment awakens you to it.

Though it is not always obvious, your body is constantly feeding you data. Even when you meet a new person, your body will either expand or contract. Pay attention to your body language the next time you are with someone and see if your shoulders are relaxed, your heart center opens, and your general energy feels relaxed—that is your body's way of giving you the spiritual thumbs up. If you feel your shoulders curl inward, and your body tense up a bit, it's giving you a "no." You can even use this simple test when it comes to

making all sorts of decisions in your life. Just place your hands on your heart and visualize yourself in the situation and feel how your body responds. In the framework of food, picture yourself going out to the dinner you had planned for tonight and eating a particular dish, and visualize how that dining experience sits with your body.

Through these exercises and practices, you are developing a relationship to your divine vehicle. You will get to know the ins and outs of how your body likes to send you its subtle messages, and the more you start listening to those signals, the clearer they will become for you. When I first started learning how to talk to my body, I felt lost. I didn't know where to begin. I relied heavily on being a detective and just noticing how I felt after certain foods or after certain exercises or varying amounts of sleep. I learned what it liked through trial and error. It took me months of following the clues to finally make some headway in my own body "case," mostly because I didn't even think to ask. I remember gorging myself on a full batch of chocolate chip cookies one night and feeling absolutely terrible. My stomach hurt, and I was so ashamed of my behavior. All of those old nasty voices will quickly return if you don't put them in check:

"You are disgusting."

"You have no self-control."

"This is why you will never have a good body."

"Go on a fast. Don't eat tomorrow. It'll balance it out."

But I noticed something that was very different this time. I knew that the thoughts weren't ME. There was a separation, and I could suddenly see those voices for what they were. I could see how hurtful they were now. I broke down and apologized. I apologized to my body, and I apologized to myself. *I don't know why I do this to you. I know you are hurting right now. I don't want to get back into this cycle. Please help me.*

In a way, talking to your body can be likened to talking to the universe or to God, depending on your belief system. They are all connected in my eyes. I sat in silence until I heard a gentle voice inside me say, *It's okay. Forgive yourself. You will know better next time.*

A wave of relief washed over me as I made silent amends to myself. *Go drink some water. Take a walk tomorrow and just be kind to yourself, okay? You are doing great.*

I think each person's experience talking to his or her body will be unique, but after spending years giving all the power and control to the voice in my head that was mean and judgmental, I was more than ready to accept this gentle, loving voice that was reminding me that I was doing great and worthy of forgiveness.

Forget the Labels and Just Listen

Although I have described my post-stomach pain diet as vegan- and gluten-free—because that's an easy concept for people to understand—I have never felt very connected to either label. In fact, to this day, one of my personal body love mantras that I share with my clients is to forget the labels and just listen.

If you feel super empowered and energized by a particular diet, such as paleo, vegan, or Mediterranean, then go for it if it feels good and works for your personal physicality. As someone who came from a place of restriction, I believe labels may set pre-established guidelines that stop you from listening and communicating with your body. I have great freedom in knowing that I can eat anything I want, that nothing is off-limits, and that I can come to my plate each day with deep love and acceptance. That label-free mentality has led to choices for my highest good and keeps me effortlessly plant-based without feeling I'm missing out on something.

It's why I don't preach a specific diet. I work with people all over the world with all kinds of eating preferences, and I would never dream of pushing a specific diet on any of them. My role is to stimulate a conversation so grounded in deep love and respect that they receive the guidance they need to fuel their bodies for optimal performance each and every day. I have complete and utter confidence in each one of your bodies to lead you along the path to radiant health and the foods that will help you get there.

The Crave Cure

If you are anything like I once was, you believe your cravings are the archenemy in the battle for a healthy, vibrant body. Even until just a few years ago, I used to abhor my cravings, but being in a loving, open relationship with my body meant that I needed to listen and interpret my cravings. I didn't want to deprive myself of what it felt like my body was asking for, because I had spent many years ignoring those kinds of cravings from a place of self-hatred. So when I had a French-fry craving that wouldn't go away, I honored it, and I ended up ordering them from an amazing little place in the East Village called Pomme Frites every single night for a week. It was getting a little ridiculous after the week was up, and I wanted to get to the root of a craving this powerful, so I decided to have a little intervention with myself. I closed my eyes and put my hands on my heart and asked my body what it *really* wanted.

As I listened quietly, all of sudden it all made sense. My body didn't want me to eat greasy French fries for dinner every single night. It just wanted something grounding. It was craving root vegetables—like potatoes—to feel balanced and centered during the freezing NYC winter. It was me who automatically interpreted this request as fries because I hadn't recently been in the habit of eating root vegetables like carrots, beets, or potatoes. Sure enough, I switched my French fries for hearty dinners that included roasted carrots or thinly sliced roasted potatoes and started feeling better immediately, while all those French fry cravings vanished instantly.

Communicating with our bodies isn't always simple and direct. Sometimes we have to do a bit of decoding, particularly when it comes to our cravings, because our mind will go to the **most readily available example**. If you take the time to break down your cravings, you will realize the essence of your body's needs. A good way to do this is by asking yourself what about consuming that particular food would make you feel good? This usually gets down to the source of the craving. And instead of leaping to the easiest solution—to your craving (which would certainly explain why it's so easy for us to repeat patterns)—think about a few alternatives to those cravings that might help, and try those on for size.

One-Size-Fits-All Nutrition

I believe in bio-individuality, meaning that we each have a unique combination of factors (genetic, environmental, etc.) that makes us process nutrients and digest foods differently. Our bio-individuality determines what we need to eat, and the amount of water, rest, and exercise we need to look and feel our absolute best. And it's precisely why I don't believe in one-size-fits-all nutrition. I will provide a wealth of delicious and practical plant-based recipes for everyone to begin his or her own journey of eating with intention. It's my

deepest intent to empower you to make your own rules, to throw away the labels, and to allow your body to ask for what it needs on a moment-to-moment basis, so you can take the highest level of care for your body. That is why—above everything—I hope you read this book and close it with the knowledge of how to go inside yourself and uncover your own specific formula for incredible health and energy.

PILLAR 4: FALL IN LOVE WITH FOOD

If you have ever been on a diet, a meal plan, a juice cleanse, or anything similar, then the idea of falling in love with your food probably feels a little dangerous. It almost certainly feels foreign. Food isn't our friend; it's this obstacle that we need to navigate strategically so we can achieve our desired body goals, right? When you think of loving food, you might even go so far as to think of one of those reality shows like *My 600-lb Life* where you spend an hour tearing up over a story of someone who has lost control of his or her relationship with food—and it might terrify you. It certainly terrified me. I have always loved food, but I always felt that enjoying food was some kind of evil urge that needed to be kept under control at all times. I could not unleash it, or it might completely destroy me. I had automatically connected loving and enjoying my food with being extremely overweight and unhealthy, so I could not understand the joy of eating intentionally. In my junior year of college, I had a completely uneventful protein shake in the morning, egg whites with steamed vegetables for lunch, and grilled chicken with more steamed vegetables for dinner. It was purely utilitarian, and I didn't enjoy a single bite of it. I never bothered to add new things or get creative in the kitchen because food was the enemy, and our relationship was strictly business.

After years of creative practice, however, I am delighted to tell you that there is a better way. You can fall in love with food that is both delicious *and* nourishes your body . . . and it doesn't have to be egg whites and steamed vegetables for every meal! When you practice tremendous gratitude and love for your body, when you start a conscious conversation to navigate its needs and decode its cravings, and when you treat your body like the precious gift it is, something magical happens. You start to fall in love with the act of fueling it.

Sacred Cooking

When I started eliminating foods, I kept my meals pretty basic, and I got extremely bored of the super simple, not-so-exciting meals I was eating. At the time, I hadn't the faintest idea how to cook vegetables beyond the steam bags I was buying regularly at the Big Y. I decided that I would embark on a little project to get to know some of the vegetables I had never cooked before. So each time I went to the supermarket, I would try one or two new vegetables to bring back to my kitchen and experiment with for the week. The key here is that I would always buy a couple of each vegetable so I could try different things, fail occasionally, and figure out what I liked best.

It was in that little yellow kitchen in my tiny off-campus apartment that I accidentally stumbled upon the act of sacred cooking, and I have never looked back. Making your kitchen a sacred space is a key part of eating with intention. In fact it was one of the first videos I made for season 1 of *Eat with Intention TV* because it's such an important element to a more loving, intentional relationship with food. Your kitchen is where it all begins: it's where you can create the food that can heal, nourish, and energize.

So how do you get into the swing of sacred cooking? For starters, you want to make your kitchen a positive place for you. Your kitchen doesn't need to look like a feature in *Martha Stewart Living*, but if you have messy cabinets or cluttered counters that give you anxiety, then you might need to do some cleaning. What matters

most is that when you walk into your kitchen, you are filled with a sense of joy. For me, this means clean counters, cute measuring cups, and a bright white kitchen flooded with daylight. For years, I couldn't swing the big white kitchen with lots of windows, but I still made my tiny kitchen feel more desirable by keeping it clean and tidy, having fresh flowers on the windowsill, and really appreciating the light that did come in. The key is to work with what you have! It can be something as simple as buying pretty colored oven mitts and dish towels to extend some of your personality to your kitchen. If your kitchen feels overstocked, cluttered, or off-balance, try a full cabinet and fridge clean-out. After you finish, you will feel lighter in every sense, and it will encourage you to get in the kitchen and make delicious food.

By infusing the whole preparation process with love, you will inevitably infuse your food with love. When I cook, I create an experience by giving my full, undivided attention to the process. I set the mood by playing Kundalini mantras or a fun, upbeat playlist, depending on my mood and the day. I get all the ingredients I want to play with, as well as some other unexpected ingredients (in case the inspiration to use them strikes). I prepare my brightly colored mixing bowls, my decorative whale-motif measuring cups, and my gold anchor spoons, all of which bring their own

special fun and energy to the process. And then I just dive in and stay really present with each step. You will never find me talking on the phone, because I refuse to prepare food on autopilot. I promise that if you do this, meal preparation becomes its own meditation. When you're chopping vegetables, be with the vegetable, stay present for the chopping, and give yourself over to this process. When sautéing, stay there with the spatula in your pan. If other thoughts or worries pop up, just redirect your focus back to the pan, back to the cooking. It's an entirely new way of preparing food, but it will bring a whole new level of deliciousness to your meals and inner peace.

Just the other day, when my assistant was fumbling around my kitchen looking for a snack, I offered her a new dairy-free, soy-free Greek "yogurt" that I was testing with gluten-free granola. She accepted and I watched her peel back the top on the yogurt and stir in the granola. I stopped her.

"You don't have to eat it out of the container like that. Grab one of the pretty bowls from the cabinet and put the yogurt and granola in there. I also have some nuts, seeds, coconut flakes, and berries in the fridge if you want to get creative with it. Make yourself a nice little bowl."

Can you imagine the difference in the experience of eating that same yogurt and granola snack? Eating yogurt sprinkled with granola out of a tiny plastic container is a mediocre food experience at best, even if you eat it with a lot of love and mindfulness. Take the little extra effort to put it all in a nice bowl and bring some love and care into making it look beautiful and delicious—it feels like a different meal to sit down and enjoy. You will feel more nourished and satisfied later.

This is why I believe Instagram has done a great service, in some ways, for food. Many people feel unsatisfied with healthy options and uninspired by clean meals because they slop them together without love and care for the presentation. The smoothie bowl trend is the perfect example of this. What once was a greenish-brown liquid to consume before your morning workout has been transformed to a gorgeous bowl with granola, superfood sprinkles, berries, bananas—all working harmoniously in an eye-catching design. I love this dressed-up version of the smoothie! The presentation of your food matters, even if you're making a quick breakfast for one. Take the extra 30 seconds to make it beautiful.

I upload a lot of my dishes on Instagram, because people love to see what I'm eating; however, I can honestly tell you that meals prepared for myself after a long day of work are the most special to me, and they look just as photogenic as the pictures I post. When you put effort into plating your food, you create an intention of reverence and respect for the food you ingest. It takes you out of the pattern of unconsciously shoveling food into your mouth and brings you back to the present and the sacredness of fueling yourself.

"When you put effort into plating your food, you create an intention of reverence and respect for the food you ingest."

Eating Mindfully

This leads me right into mindful, intentional eating. This is surprisingly just a small part of a much larger process. Once you've begun to practice some of my rituals and exercises—such as developing a healthy sense of gratitude and acceptance for your body, eating from a place of self-love, and having an on-going dialogue with your body—mindful eating just happens! If you are already connected and in tune with the process, mindful eating becomes a default setting. Magic, right?

Want to delve deeper? Set specific intentions for your food at every meal and engage in conscious chewing practices to make your eating even more mindful. Sit down, close the laptop, put the phone away, and focus on your food. When you are eating, you should eat without distractions. Eat with purpose. Take the time to engage with your food and savor each bite. Your stomach doesn't have teeth, so chewing your food well will improve digestion and keep you in the present moment with the delicious meal in front of you. If you are naturally a quick eater, break the cycle by putting your fork down after each bite, and then finish chewing before you pick it up again. Establishing the space and time to be with and enjoy your food will slow you down and allow you to value the experience.

The recipes in this book are also designed to engage you in a mindful experience with what's on your plate. Each recipe has its own assigned mantra, which is purposefully paired with a specific meditation or mindfulness exercise. You may use them any way you want, but I've made a few suggestions below.

• One approach is to choose a recipe from this book that appeals to you, prepare the dish, and then read the meditation. Ponder it. Entertain the idea that perhaps being drawn to that specific recipe was indeed a way to bring you to that message.

• This exercise is for those seeking inspiration from the message. If you want to be "open to unexpected opportunities," then turn to the recipe that holds that intention (in this case, page 175) and utilize the corresponding meditation and mantra to create a ritual to put forth that intention and enjoy its accompanying recipe. You can read the meditation in the morning before you start cooking or in the evening after you've finished.

• My favorite approach is to use the book like a tarot deck or oracle. Close your eyes with the book in hand and ask for guidance. Then open your book randomly to a page and receive whatever message and meal is waiting for you.

If you have been practicing the exercises as you read along, you have become more mindful of your eating habits—noting the foods you select and paying attention to the way you feel afterward. One key way to eating mindfully is to ask yourself before each meal whether or not you are eating from a place a self-love or self-sabotage. Like I discussed on page 33, you can eat a kale salad from either a place of love and nourishment so that your body can be fueled or from a place of deep self-loathing and of wishing your body would change. Your intention and the energy behind your reasons for eating that salad greatly affect your body's ability to digest it. Don't believe me? Think about a time when you were particularly upset or stressed out, and even though you were eating the same normal foods you always eat, all of a sudden they were going right through you. When we are in certain emotional and energetic states, our bodies have a much harder time digesting food. The energy with which you eat can certainly affect the way your body processes that food.

So what should you do when you're eating something from a place of self-sabotage and not self-love? You have already made it past the first step, which is to have a conversation with yourself as to why you are eating what's on your plate. Now that you're honest with yourself, you can choose to see things differently and that can go one of two ways. In the first way, you might acknowledge that you are eating the food in front of you in a self-sabotaging manner, because you don't love your body in its current state and you want it to be skinnier. Try to take a moment to sit back and search for that place of gratitude for your body. Once you achieve that, THEN decide to continue with your food from a place of self-awareness. This small acknowledgment is enough to cause a shift in your intention and energy around the food. The second way—and what I recommend doing when you're first starting out—is to ask yourself if the food in front of you is what you really want. Ask yourself, "If I fully loved and accepted my body, what would I have in this moment?" and then give yourself permission to have it if that is truly what you would have in the moment. The surprising thing with this question is that sometimes you will hear your body telling you that it wants the smoothie, other times you will hear that it wants a more substantial breakfast. I love asking that question because even if it's just a hypothetical, you are pausing in the moment and tuning in to the energy of what it would feel like to genuinely love and accept your body. Keep practicing and building that self-love!

> "Ask yourself before each meal whether or not you're eating from a place of self-love."

When you eat from a place of self-love, you bring more awareness around your specific intention for that meal: nourishment, healing, or energy. When you make something and **eat it with the intention of genuine nourishment**, it can have a profound effect on your body's reaction to that food so, of course, it also helps to know which foods naturally support our beautiful bodies.

CHAPTER 2

The Well-Being Trifecta

I arrived at a crossroad on my professional journey about three years ago. There was one platform focused on healthy eating and fueling my body, but there was also a spiritual side that championed self-love and listening to my intuition. I believed wholeheartedly in both ideas, but I felt like I had to choose which side to really take a stand on professionally. So I did what I do when I'm feeling torn and I went inside. I meditated with the intention of gaining clarity around which path to take, and then I journaled to see what came to light. And like a lightning bolt, it hit me hard.

It's all the same. The self-love, the body acceptance, the eating properly, the listening to your intuition, the fueling and caring for both your physical and your spiritual self are ALL part of the whole. Food, meditation, and self-care are all essential components of this whole, so we need to embrace all of them if we want to look, feel, and live our best in this lifetime.

So I want you to really let this sink in. I call this our "well-being trifecta," and it incorporates food, meditation, and self-care as a sacred triangle anchoring the best version of you. They are inseparable to eat with intention, and you should honor and utilize all three of them collectively to fully tap into their individual powers.

Take food and meditation, for example. If you're fueling your body with junk food, you can still receive the many benefits of meditation and tap into your intuition; however, you will only experience a fraction of your potential. Why? Because when you eat processed foods, junk food, or even foods that disagree with your body, you create a reaction inside of you that shuts off your higher senses. If you don't believe me, do a test on yourself. Eat a light dinner filled with greens, have a green juice the next morning, and then meditate for twenty minutes. The next day, have a pizza for dinner and a brownie for dessert, and then eat a bowl of cereal the next morning. Then "try" to meditate, because I suspect that it will be a challenge just to retain the focus to sit down in stillness! When I tried it, my mind was racing a million miles a minute, and I struggled to hear any intuitive guidance. I reached a new level of operating once I realized that my dietary choices affected my focus.

When we clean up our diet, we clear out our minds. When we stop using food as emotional comfort or punishment, we bring it back to its highest purpose—fuel—and we start eating in a way that supports our greater good. Similarly, if you eat nourishing foods with love for your body but ignore your self-care needs, you will feel as though you're physically and mentally deteriorating. We have all been there: pulling crazy hours, not sleeping enough, and eating poorly. I have also personally test-driven down the other road and it is just as bad—I can be juicing or making fresh vegetable-laden meals, but I cannot function at my highest level if my body is aching for rest and requires self-care.

And even if you are having bubble baths, getting enough rest, and going for long, leisure strolls in the park, you should still meditate. While all of those activities do wonders for your mental state and happiness, there is nothing more powerful than sitting down to meditate and reaching deep inside for guidance and connecting with the truth of who you are. These three practices are inseparable and essential if you really want to blow the ceiling off what you think is possible.

SELF-CARE

When I was very young, I became ill and went from playing street hockey and soccer to barely being able to get off the couch. It was terrifying—I didn't know what was wrong with me, but it suddenly felt as though life was being sucked out of me. The doctors finally concluded that I had mononucleosis and that it needed to run its course. I was sent home and instructed to sleep and drink plenty of fluids, and so I did.

Since then, I've developed profound awareness of my energy levels, which is something that I don't think a lot of children think about. I witnessed firsthand the healing power of listening to your body, allowing it to sleep, and giving it the fluids it needs to thrive. It was about three months of doctor visits and various medications, and the best thing they ever did was to just take me off of all of it and let me sleep. That experience taught me that I needed more sleep than most people and when I ignored my body's signals for rest, my body would shut down on me.

These days, I have a much more peaceful relationship with my body. I take baths almost every single night ever since I discovered that my body loves warm water with lavender Epsom salts. I can almost feel it saying "thank you" to me every time I relax into the tub. I have also become an occasional napper. I used to push through or caffeinate myself through a tired spell, but now I realize that my body tells me what it needs. When I listen to my body and just give in to the nap, I wake up an hour or so later, completely refreshed to jump into the next task of the day. Self-care is no different than food. When you love and accept your body, you begin to hear its requests for rest, relaxation, and rejuvenation. Whether it be bubble baths, painting, a cup of herbal tea, reading book, or listening to music, indulge in that one thing that relaxes you at the end of the day and puts you in a good head space.

FOOD

Unsurprisingly, it was the keen awareness of my energy levels that convinced me of my newly cleaned-up diet. As you read in chapter 1, the high level of energy I felt after the first couple of weeks alone made me a believer for life.

I immediately realized that the foods I consumed could be measured in other ways beyond the number on a scale. I was absolutely fascinated by the changes in my mind and body. After abstaining from meat and dairy, I was noticeably less moody, and my periods were much less painful.

Finally, I had more energy, and I was off the emotional food roller coaster that had terrorized me for so long. I was grateful and overwhelmed with those two developments alone that I could barely wrap my head around the idea that there might be more. Years later, as a vegan, gluten-free baking enthusiast, I read about the effects of sugar on our bodies and minds, and I decided to omit bread and sugary baked goods from my diet and see what happened. Well, as you might have guessed, I had more sustained energy and sharper focus instead of sporadic energy bursts, which are synonymous with sugar. I didn't even realize how distracted and scattered I had been before I quit sugar. Oh, and as an added bonus, my acne cleared up. I had struggled with facial acne since puberty, had tried every cream and wash on the market, and despite my best efforts, I could not keep my skin clear. And just like that, it was gone! After just a few weeks of giving up all processed carbs and sugar, my skin looked the best it ever had in my adult life.

Don't get my wrong: I have not sworn off bread or sugar. I love bread as much as the next person, but it's no longer a part of my daily life because it doesn't love me (with or without gluten). Occasionally, when I'm in the mood for toast or pizza with gluten-free dough, I go for it. When I was in Paris, you bet I had a croissant. I am all about LIVING, and it's the reason that I never put bread totally off-limits. Everyone is different in this area, so again, it's really about knowing your-self. If having a little bread means you consume an entire loaf, then skip it. For someone like me who came from such a restrictive dietary background, this little opening gives me freedom and grants me choice every day because I care about my body's needs.

The great news about the food conversation with your body is that you will get into the swing of listening to its needs and responding to it so intuitively that it becomes integrated into your life-style. You do NOT have to spend the rest of your life writing in a food-mood journal. You reprogram yourself to veer toward foods that fuel you and to listen to your intuition when it says, "Meh, not feeling anymore kale this week." So many of us waste precious energy stressing out about what food to eat, how much we should have, and if we should try this or that diet. I used to be totally consumed by it and it was not a fun place to live. This whole process is getting you out of your head about food and back into your life so that you can experience a whole new level of living!

MEDITATION

Meditation has been the most epic of game changers for my life. People meditate for various reasons: to release work stress, to seek peace of mind, or to establish a deeper connection with God or another spiritual entity. I found meditation because I didn't know how to live after my brother was diagnosed with a rare terminal illness that was eating away at his organs (see page 8). I've already explained how meditation transformed my life, but I don't want you think that meditation is just for a certain type of person—meditation can help *everyone*.

I remember being with Kenny in the hospital after his large intestine was removed, and the inflammation in his body had reached new heights. We were walking laps around the nurses' station to build up his strength post-surgery when his vitals went crazy. We didn't understand what was going on, just that the big monitor he was attached to started beeping, but the nurse came and said that he needed to go back to his room immediately because his vitals were dangerously high enough to send him into cardiac arrest. When we returned to his room, I said to him, "Kenny, sit down and close your eyes. I know you are not into this stuff, but just humor me right now and listen along." He did as I instructed, and I led him through a very simple meditation to try and slow his vitals. And within a few minutes, a nurse rushed in and asked us, "What are you doing in here? His vitals suddenly look gorgeous." Kenny's heart rate had returned to normal in just minutes, and he wasn't even a believer when I had him do it. For me, that afternoon was a victory on so many levels, the least of which had showed my little brother firsthand the effects of meditation in a language he could process, with numbers and science. It has made me even more passionate about spreading the benefits of meditation. You don't need to be spiritual to enjoy it—it can work miracles on *anyone* who is ready and willing to learn.

When I first began meditating, I felt as if I had entered a vortex. All I had done was show up, willing and desperate to find a way to calm my mind and connect to something inside of me for strength, and the gates just opened. In fact, you would be amazed by how far a little willingness goes! If you have had enough; if you are done feeling imprisoned by food and your body; and if you are ready for guidance to help you navigate from where you are to where you want to be, then you are ready for meditation in your life. I am so proud of you for having the courage to say *enough.* For admitting that you can't continue this way any longer and for surrendering, because THAT is where the magic happens. It's an honor to guide you through this journey because I've lived it, and I'm committed to helping you navigate it even more gracefully, with more ease and less pain and in much less time than I did!

I like to tell my clients to think about meditation as medication. The amount of medication you take for a minor headache will differ from the amount you need if your leg were cut off. So if you try to heal a devastating wound (like mine when my brother was diagnosed), you probably need a stronger "dosage." I believe it was my willingness to engulf myself in meditation that saved my life, but any amount of daily meditation will bring you tremendous results and improve the quality of your life.

I am also a big advocate of a daily practice, which we will get into deeper in chapter 5, when you learn how to integrate all these practices and new choices into your life. Even if it's just for one minute a day, start where you are comfortable, but don't be afraid to turn up your practice to correspond with your current needs.

After a month or so of meditating, my life began to shift before my eyes—I was doing things that brought me joy. I started looking for activities and people that lit me up during this time. I found myself going to more Kundalini classes, writing more, and spending a lot of time in the kitchen baking and cooking for my blog. I have to stress that this wasn't a luxury at this time in my life: it was a survival strategy. I didn't have much money at all, and I was still acting to pay the bills, but I could not wait to get home and take pictures for my blog or post a new YouTube video. I would get lost in the magic, be swept away by just the doing of these things.

I suppose it helped me balance out the hard times. It's not that I stopped crying or feeling sad about my brother; in fact, that journey continues to this day. I have moments—even days—of deep, dark sadness about his condition. When Kenny went into surgery to remove his large intestine, I would sit in easy pose on the floor of the hospital chapel, crying hysterically, and bargaining with God. That brought me more comfort than anything else could during those scariest few hours of my life. It wasn't about pretending my feelings weren't there, it was feeling held by a power much greater than me while experiencing them. However, the joy that I'm ruthlessly committed to in the remaining aspects of my life help me weather those bad storms—the storms that matter.

This triangle of well-being has been my saving grace and my anchor to hold down my ship during the storm, but it has also been my rocket ship, propelling me to a life beyond my wildest dreams. I truly believe it is the secret sauce to living a life that LIGHTS you up from the inside out. It doesn't serve us to pretend that bad things don't happen in the world or in our lives; it's not helping you to ignore the patterns that are hurting you or the feelings that well deep in your soul from events that have happened in your life, but that doesn't mean any of those things need to take us out of the game.

> "It doesn't serve us to pretend that bad things don't happen in our lives."

This life is a gift—it's a precious privilege to walk this Earth, so let's really live while we are here. When the world throws us a curveball, we don't have to feel out of control. We have the power to take a deep breath, recenter, go back into our "toolbox," and navigate ourselves to safe shores. By cultivating this trifecta as the base of our operating, we achieve altitude in all aspects of our lives: the ability to look at circumstances from above and have some peace, clarity, and compassion.

See, eating with intention is not just about you looking amazing in your favorite red dress. It clears your mind and gives you open access to a whole new level of living—a level where you feel energized to wake up each day, where you LOVE your life, and where you go to bed at night feeling wrapped in gratitude for another day of wonder. It's a level that is pretty impossible to

access when you spend your time counting calories, thinking horrible things about your body, and feeling foggy and stressed out.

Now that you are on your way to feeling great, loving your body, and listening to your inner guidance, let's talk about how you can utilize all that goodness to totally transform your life.

BUILDING A FOUNDATION FOR EXPANSION

Intention: Design the infrastructure to hold all the beautiful things you are ready to have in your life.

Every skyscraper needs a solid foundation before it can soar to incredible heights, and if you are ready to build a life beyond your wildest dreams, then you need to become a container that can hold that reality. This is something often overlooked by people who want to do big things in the world, attract immense wealth, or have a whirlwind romance that turns into the love of their life. Do you honestly have the infrastructure in place to handle that if it came to you right now? I certainly didn't at first. I would be offered a ridiculously well-paid project, but I wouldn't manage the wealth properly or invest in myself to get better gigs. Or I would be on a wellness kick, and then fall in love and suddenly skip yoga classes or eat poorly, so I didn't seem too high-maintenance to my new boyfriend. I'll save you the trouble of guessing how things turned out.

It never works. You always lose because it's not sustainable.

I've gone down that path and it has led me to a place that I refuse to return to. Those experiences of poor money management and ignoring my own needs helped me realize that I needed to build the infrastructure to support my desired life. I needed to be clear about my income and expenses, so I hired a bookkeeper and opened several bank accounts. Now I properly distribute my wealth as soon as it comes in knowing that it goes to the investments and funds to fuel my biggest life. I even have "fun" and "education" accounts because I value both. I want to stress that I built this infrastructure before there was a great amount of money coming in, but I firmly believe it sent the message to the universe that I was ready for the responsibility, and it certainly allowed me to sustain a new level of finances when they did come.

When it came to love, I took time to create a solid daily routine based around my highest priorities so that my building was so strong that when the next tornado (or boyfriend) hit, I would not be swayed. This, for me, is daily meditation, food that makes me feel good, enough alone time to reflect and refresh, and the freedom to shine my brightest and do the work I'm here to do in the world. Making my priorities a pillar in my life also quickly illuminated men who were not aligned with what I truly wanted, which was both a tremendous blessing and a time-saver. When you show up for yourself, you can show up better for everyone in your life, period.

FOLLOWING YOUR INTERNAL COMPASS: DAILY MEDITATION

Intention: *All of the answers are inside. You just have to learn how to listen to them.*

Here's where a daily meditation practice comes in handy. All of us have access to our intuitive knowing; however, few of us create an environment for ourselves to actually listen to it. It is famously said that praying is when you ask for guidance and meditation is when you listen to receive it. Now, don't let the word "praying" throw you off if you are not particularly religious—the asking can be in any manner with which you feel comfortable. You can journal down a question before your meditation (I love doing this),

or simply set the intention before your practice within yourself, saying, "I would like to receive clarity around project X and what are the next steps I should take." And, of course, you also pray to whichever deity you wish, be it God or Elvis. The important part is that you are *asking*, you are opening up a conversation with something beyond. The asking is like a sweet, little surrender—a beautiful thing. You are giving up whatever the situation may be to a power greater than you or to your highest self (the part of you that's all-knowing). This creates the space for miracles to occur.

Any kind of meditation practice works, so commit to one. Try out the different meditations in this book to see what you are naturally drawn to and what feels good, and stick to it for 40 days straight before moving on to a new meditation. You can start with just a few minutes (I recommend trying 3 minutes to start if you have never done it before, but even 1 minute is a start), and gradually build up to 20 or more. Consistency is key, so choose something that you are willing to do daily. By clearing our minds and going into that peaceful place each day, we pump up the volume on our internal compass. This way, when you have a decision to make or are unclear on the next step, you have your internal GPS system ready to pipe up and lovingly guide you to the choice that's most aligned with your highest good.

A beautiful thing happens when you can hear your internal guidance system. You stop needing to ask everyone in your life his or her opinion about everything. Here's the thing, the people in your life love you and want what's best for you, but at the end of the day, only you truly know what the best move is for you. Many people can get trapped in this cycle. They create the space through meditation and receive clear direction or gut feelings, but then second-guess it by asking for everyone's opinion. As a result, the person is even more confused than when he or she started. Sounds exhausting, right? It is. Trust yourself.

Daily meditation helps you get to your destination much faster, which means you can go farther and hit more places than you would if you allowed yourself to get stuck in the hamster wheel of indecision. Plus, listening to your internal compass is just like building a muscle. At first, it will feel a little uncomfortable and you may not feel strong or confident, but with practice and daily reps, your intuition muscle will grow larger, and you can hold more weight.

The most successful way to build this muscle is to engage your internal GPS in every tiny decision for at least 2 weeks. That means you should meditate daily, but it also means you should tune in to your intuition for every decision you make. For example, should you go to that event your friend invited you to tonight? Take a moment, get quiet, and ask yourself, "Does this feel expansive?" and "Is going to this for my highest good?"

> "Your intuition or internal guidance never speaks in 'shoulds.'"

Listen to what you hear. It's likely at first that it will be a soft feeling you will be tempted to ignore. Perhaps in this case, you realize immediately that it doesn't feel as expansive as staying home and getting some rest would be, but then another voice chimes in, " . . . but you should go because what if there's a good networking opportunity there?" Listen to the first, less "logical" voice. Your intuition or internal guidance never speaks in "shoulds," so that's always a dead give-away. You can trust that if there were someone you were supposed to meet at that event that you would feel excited and expansive about going. I realize that may be hard to trust at first, but that's why this exercise is so important. I have full confidence that after truly utilizing it, you will build up a deep respect and reverence for your own inner knowing.

CHAPTER 3

Shifting Your Habits

"Anytime you're gonna grow, you're gonna lose something. You're losing what you're hanging onto to keep safe. You're losing habits that you're comfortable with, you're losing familiarity."

—James Hillman

Being uncomfortable in the new habits you are creating is just part of the skin you are shedding. Those habits were keeping you safe, but they were also keeping you small. Although it can feel really funky and weird at first, it's time to spread your wings. I mean, you have spent your whole life walking on two feet, and now you're trying on flying for size. There is going to be a learning curve. I urge you to enjoy it! Laugh through it. Be so kind to yourself during this transition. You are retraining your mind and your body.

I totally get that these patterns and habits you have around food and your body will not vanish overnight. After all, you have been solidifying those thought patterns for years at this point, and they will try to hold on for dear life! Luckily, with persistent effort and consciousness around your behaviors, you will rewrite those old patterns and build new muscles every day until they will be your first instinct! Here, I share some tools in maintaining this new way of life.

BUILDING THE NEW

Socrates once said, "The secret to change is to focus all of your energy, not on fighting the old, but on building the new." I am such a firm believer in this, and I think it explains the failure of prohibitive diets. You focus so much on the food you *can't* have and the things you are trying to change about the old you that you're not looking forward. You're not looking to the new. While you may still want to eliminate a food because of a food allergy or because it's not working with your body, you will come to that conclusion organically on your own by eating with intention. If you eliminate a food, it is still a good idea to put your attention to the foods you *can* eat. Take a little time and find new recipes for the meals that make you feel good.

This was a revelation for me when I first shifted the food I was eating, and it was paramount to me not to feel deprived. I felt like a painter with a new set of paints when I started cooking with new ingredients. It was exhilarating to cook now because it challenged me to think outside of the box. My energy wasn't spent lamenting over all the food sacrifices I was making or complaining about how hard it was to *not* eat the ice cream or the pizza; it was all directed toward finding new, creative ways to cook the foods that made me feel great. I'd buy a couple of new "first time" vegetables each week and make it my business to find at least one delicious way to cook them. My energy was focused on building the new that the old, naturally and painlessly, disappeared!

This concept goes beyond food and can be applied to every area of your life. Maybe you want to stop nagging or pestering your partner about the small things, and you want to be more loving and supportive in your relationship. Direct your energy toward being the kind of partner you *want to be* rather than giving all of your energy to walking on eggshells and holding your tongue all the time. Or if you want to reduce your stress at work, think of ways to bring joy and fun into your work instead of how you can "combat" the stress. When we focus on what we want to create, the whole process flows with so much more ease and pleasure.

WHEN SHOULD I STOP EATING A FOOD ALTOGETHER?

At times, abstinence is required when it comes to eating habits, and it's a useful tool if you feel out of control in handling your eating. I had no trouble limiting gluten in my life: I have bread occasionally, and it makes it easier for me to avoid it knowing that I can indulge once in a while. Sugar, on the other hand, was my guilty pleasure and required abstinence. When I eat a little bit, I can barely stop myself from eating it five more times that day. If I bake cookies that aren't sugar-free, I will eat them all. They don't stand a chance.

Some of you reading this might think I'm a little nutty, but I bet many of you are nodding with empathy. It was a defining moment when I saw that I had a problem. I'm sure there are a lot of people who can have one cookie and be totally fine and go about eating normally for the rest of the day. That person is not me. (Though I can eat just a few potato chips without devouring a whole bag!)

The trick is to know what foods trigger you, what foods stir up addictive behaviors in you, or lead you further down that destructive rabbit hole. These foods are *not* your friends. Can you think of anything you're currently eating that has this kind of effect on you? If you think you know your "trigger" foods, jot them down in your food-mood journal. Pay some extra attention to them this week and observe your patterns around these foods, so you can make an executive decision about whether or not you need to abstain from them altogether.

It's important to be brutally honest with yourself during this process. Do some journaling and let it all out; release your feelings around these foods that sabotage you and feed destructive patterns. Be nice to yourself around this. You are not weird, you are not weak, you are human—and you are so incredibly brave and courageous for having the fortitude to look at yourself and your habits to make self-improvements. Besides, you are ready to rewrite that programming!

Cold Turkey

Once you've identified your problem foods, what next? Do you really need to go cold turkey and give it up completely? That is truly up to you to decide. Some people find it easier to give it all up at once, cut off the drug, so to speak. You can also take a progressive approach if that's easier. If your trigger food is sugar, start off by just eliminating added sugar (like the kind you might put in your coffee) and sweet treats like cupcakes and cookies. Once you begin to feel comfortable, you can get more specific and read the labels of all your groceries and avoid anything with sneaky "dried cane syrup" in there. I've found it in almond milk, granola, salad dressings, and other foods I thought were clean of it. Also, pay closer attention to your reactions around fruit that is higher in sugar, like mangoes and grapes. Doing it in two stages may also lessen the pain of the detox, which can be pretty intense if you are used to eating a lot of sugar.

When you begin abstaining from a certain food—whether it's all at once or in steps—it's important to be kind to yourself during the transition. Take lots of baths, get plenty of rest, and really honor what your body needs. Drink water with lemon on a daily basis to help support your body to quickly flush out any toxins. Eat lots of

healthy fats to feel full. Don't let yourself get to a ravenous place when you're detoxing because it's going to intensify your cravings and make the whole process that much harder. Make sure that you are eating hearty, nutritious meals that satiate you. This will also help you decipher your addictive cravings from actual hunger.

The one thing I absolutely don't recommend during this process is giving yourself a "cheat day" with your trigger food, because it will make it exponentially harder for you to abstain the remaining six days of the week and may lead you to binge on that one day. You wouldn't tell an alcoholic that it was okay to drink on Sundays, or that having one glass of wine with dinner doesn't count. You wouldn't do that because you know that their reaction to a glass of wine is different from yours. So I'm asking you to be really honest with yourself, go inside, and determine if any foods or beverages (like coffee!) make you feel this way.

Situation Triggers

Now let's take a look at your situation triggers. Some common situations or events that may induce addictive behavior include anything related to alcohol, barbecues, holidays, buffets, or certain stressful circumstances, but there are loads more and each one of us has our own special triggers. What situations lead you to abnormally excessive food consumption? Where do you feel you lose control or get caught up in a habitual pattern and feel powerless to resist?

Let's start with alcohol. When I was a freshman in college and I still had disordered behaviors around food (way before my stomach pains and plant-based lifestyle), I used to beg my then-boyfriend not to let me order food after we went out drinking. I would make him swear up and down that he was to stop me from ordering pizza no matter the circumstance. He never stood a chance. I would wake up in the morning, see the leftover boxes on the floor, and feel absolutely disgusted with myself.

Old habits die hard. My partying lessened tremendously after college, but I still indulged in a glass or two of wine with girlfriends from time to time and I was more inclined to end the night eating leftovers out of my fridge. Alcohol was a major trigger for me, and I see it with many friends and clients too. It's easy to see why: our judgment is impaired and we are not making our most intuitive choices when we are tipsy. It's not about feeling bad about having a glass of wine with dinner. It's about acknowledging where your triggers lie so you can better navigate those situations with knowledge and intention and perhaps shift your unconscious eating patterns. When you begin to incorporate these new patterns of intuitive eating, abstain from triggers such as alcohol to make it easier for you to commit to the change. With time and awareness of my meals, I was fine with an occasional glass of wine without getting derailed. Know yourself and make the choice that's going to set you up for success!

> "It's not about feeling bad about having a glass of wine with dinner."

Holidays, barbecues, and buffets are similar triggers because of the copious options and your sense of obligation to try a bit of everything. As a result, you end up eating way more then you needed and feel guilty and uncomfortable. Don't underestimate the emotional triggers at events like these, particularly during the holidays, which could lead you to eating more than you need to (read on for tips on navigating emotional triggers). When faced with a buffet, give yourself two plates. Fill your first plate up with all the salad you want, and then let the second plate be your "main course." This is a little visual trick to help your brain register that you have eaten an entire meal. Trying a little of this and a little of that with ten different tiny plates doesn't give us the visual cue to stop eating.

Emotional Eating During Stressful Times

The final trigger I want to mention is stress, and many people tend to emotionally eat during stressful situations. When I first moved to Manhattan after college, I was waitressing (so original, I know) and would come home every single night and binge on mango guacamole with pita chips. Now you might be wondering what's the big deal. It's not too unhealthy of a food.

The big deal isn't about *what* I was eating. It was the fact that I was eating it every night for stress relief. It was my *intention* for eating it and my addictive tendency with it that made it an unhealthy habit. Maybe you have a habit of stopping by that bakery on the way home from work and "treating" yourself to a red velvet cupcake when you've had a stressful day. These emotional eating patterns have become cultural norms, so we become unconscious to the fact that we have ritualized our emotional eating, and it makes us feel like it's perfectly normal. Society can even trick us into thinking it's a form of self-love, but let's be clear: this is no way an act of self-love. We try to eat away our feelings and numb the pain we are going through instead of dealing with the emotions that are coming up for us. What would happen if you actually treated yourself with some love during those rough emotional times? If you really allowed yourself to feel those feelings and asked yourself what you really needed? I guarantee that it is not Ben & Jerry's Chocolate Therapy ice cream.

Years after I had made peace with my body, I

still had a very emotional relationship with food. I began writing in my food-mood journal again and started looking at my eating patterns. I noticed a few glaringly obvious things right away. First and foremost, I was an emotional snacker. I would grab that cookie every single time I stressed out over work. I also noticed that I had fallen into patterns with go-to foods that I would order from the same few restaurants around me. It was apparent from my detective work that I had started eating on autopilot.

Meal-Planning Miracle

Enter mindful meal planning! I had never been a big meal planner. I didn't like meal plans. I preferred to eat and enjoy in the moment. However, it was clear that this wasn't really working for me during stressful times. So one day I decided to commit to planning out three solid meals the evening before. I would plan out three hearty meals to ensure that I wouldn't actually be physically hungry for a snack in between and accommodate any meals I knew I would be eating out by pre-deciding on what I was ordering. To be honest, it was a little annoying at first sitting down and planning the next day's meals out, but before I knew it, it became the new normal.

Meal planning also allowed me to eat a greater variety of foods because I took the time to plan what I was having and try new recipes. I had no idea how much time I wasted debating what I was eating on a day-to-day basis, even though I ended up making most food choices on autopilot anyway. So if you find it exhausting to constantly be debating about where to have your next meal or what to make for your next meal, plan it out the night before! Save your precious time and brain space and relax about the food.

Now, what if during the day you checked in with your body and it actually wanted something different than what you had pre-decided the night before? Well that's totally fine. Usually I am pretty spot-on with my choices, but every so often, it

happens. The night before I may have planned a nice big salad for dinner, but when the time came, I was in the mood for some warming, hearty soup because it had been freezing outside all day. As long as I checked in with myself and made sure that my substitution wasn't coming as a reaction to an emotional feeling I was having, I gave myself permission to switch out whatever I wanted. The one thing I rarely do these days is add in a snack. I know that when I am eating well-portioned, balanced meals, my body does not need snacks and my snacking tendencies are almost always emotionally fueled, so I just say no and step away from the donut!

If you want to give meal planning a whirl, I advise sticking with it for at least 40 days so you can fully adjust and see all the benefits. If possible, enlist a friend to do it with you—the two of you can even email each other your meal plans the evening before and then let each other know if you decide to make a substitution during the day. Feel free to utilize the community in the Eat with Intention online course to find a planning buddy for this as well or just share your meals with the group and we can help keep you accountable. Sometimes just telling even one other person can be the difference between keeping your word and honoring your commitment and losing steam and falling back into old patterns. Remember the mantra "know thyself and plan accordingly."

Mindful meal planning helped me stop that emotional snacking habit for good. It's been years since I had to plan out meals the night before, but I still eat three nourishing meals a day and rarely snack. Just like I went back to my original food-mood journaling to discover my emotional eating patterns, meal planning is an evergreen tool. Use them and then keep them on the shelf for later when you get stuck in a rut. They are always accessible so you are never far from getting back on track.

CHAPTER 4

Taking Care of You

A magical thing happens when we make peace with our bodies and start listening to our souls' voices (or inner GPS): we begin to feel like we are enough. That's right, just us, just being right here, in this moment, is enough. That in and of itself is a victory over so many forces in our society that profit from telling you that you need to take a pill, buy a dress, or do a style of workout to make you "worthy." You are a glorious, divine being who does not need to do anything—you simply need to sit in your being. Be the peace, the love, and the inspiration that you seek and you will draw it to you. Your energy, the way you feel each day, is your most precious commodity when you are sitting in your being. How can you let others drink from your cup when you haven't even filled it up?

Many women tend to give and give and give that we forget to also take care of ourselves. And it's hard to give someone else great energy when you are running on fumes. Somewhere in our psyche, we've managed to convince ourselves that it's selfish or indulgent to take care of ourselves, that we should feel guilty if we are not putting the needs of others before our own. I see this all the time with my coaching clients, many of whom second-guess themselves before they even take the leap to sign up. They'll email me saying, "I feel really guilty spending this money on something for me when I have two kids whom I could be spending it on." Or, "I feel guilty taking the hour a week to myself when I have a family to take care of and feel so overwhelmed to get everything done." These responses hurt my heart. I am constantly reminding women that when we take care of ourselves EVERYONE in our life benefits.

Want to know the secret to being a better mom, wife, friend, daughter, and business woman? It's making YOUR own well-being a priority.

Still feeling resistant? Hear me out. When you are well rested, well meditated, well fed, and nourished—from the tip of your toes to the crown of your head—you radiate light. When your cup is filled all the way, you can't help but let it spill over and share it with those around you. When you don't make yourself a priority and you still try to give to everyone in your life, it is nearly impossible not to feel drained, worn out, and even resentful. Let's find a way to help you make yourself a priority and honor the care your being needs to function at its highest level.

SELF-CARE

This new level of energy that you have and bring to those around you will transform your relationships on all levels. Your head will be clearer, you will be a better listener, and you will have greater vitality in life. Your partner will be so grateful for the happier, more loving version of you that he will gladly do the dishes, so that you can take a bubble bath before the two of you tuck in for the night. Trust me, once he sees the goddess that emerges after giving you a half hour of self-care, he will likely become an outspoken advocate for it. Men who send their wives off for spa days or on a girl's trip recognize the MAJOR return on their investments when their lady comes back rejuvenated and refreshed. Take a stand for your own self-care and lay it down like the law. Men can do this pretty innately that it's likely he won't bat an eye when you tell him you're heading to the spa this Sunday with the girls. (After all, his version of that would be, "The boys and I are playing basketball Thursday night. I'll be home around 9.") Men are fairly intuitive to the time they need to recharge and take it unapologetically, whether it's playing with the boys or taking a long drive. As women, our care-giving instincts can hinder our own self-care, which is why it is essential to build the muscles for incorporating self-care into our lives.

For new mothers, babies take center stage and it can be an exhausting process, so you need to get as much sleep as you can—in fact, it is in everyone's best interest to support you so that you are nourished even when you don't have time or energy to cook. Get in as many baths, naps, and sleep time as possible so that you have enough energy to actually enjoy that special time with your little one.

Self-care sets a great example for your kids. Once your children are a little older, schedule times that work for you and your family, and know that when you do take even a small amount of time to take care of yourself, you become a better version of yourself for your family because you are energized and in a better mood. Your kids may get a sliver less time with you, but I am certain they would prefer to see this self-cared side of you than the exhausted, disengaged, and low-energy side—it's to everyone's benefit when you are fully present and in the moment.

Self-care also increases the quality of your professional work. If I'm sleep deprived, low on fuel, or in need of R&R, I will not work as effectively and

efficiently as I normally do. I find it harder to write, to express myself, and to retain focus—my energy is dimmer in comparison to what it is when I'm running at full force. I know that in order for me to share my work with the world, my own inner cup needs to be overflowing so that I can give at the level I want to in the world.

So what EXACTLY is "self-care"?

> ## "Take a stand for your own self-care and lay it down like the law."

Everyone has his or her own definition of self-care, and it is often confused with self-love. Though related, self-love means love yourself, and those who do, tend to take their self-care pretty seriously. Self-care is any intentional action you take to care for your physical, mental, or emotional health. It can be anything: from the foods you put into your body to fuel it properly, getting a massage, and taking a bath to soothe sore muscles to meditating, cuddling up with a nice cup of tea and a good book, or doing an art project with a few friends in the center of your living room.

Self-care differs from loving yourself, but self-care does come more naturally when you do love and accept yourself. Once you begin to honor yourself and invest in self-care, you will discover that taking care of your most basic needs will bring out the best you, on a higher level, for everyone and everything in your life. More importantly, you also set a desperately needed example in this world.

Self-Care Sundays

I will never forget the reactions of my friends and colleagues when I started "self-care Sundays" a couple of years ago. I was worn down from my non-stop schedule and craved an entire day without a schedule, a plan, and even other people. I decided to give myself Sundays. On Sundays, I would not make plans in advance; if you wanted to hang out on a Sunday, I would be totally transparent and let you know that Sunday was my self-care day, so I never put anything on the calendar, but if I woke up on Sunday morning and felt drawn to do whatever the invitation might be for, I would absolutely give you a ring and join in. It wasn't about lazing around and whiling away Sundays; it was having an open schedule without any commitments or prearranged obligations. I spent a lot of Sundays strolling around the farmers' market (wearing something that very closely resembled pajamas), purchasing my bounty for the week from the same familiar faces, and ordering an almond milk latte from my favorite little East Village café. I'd take a leisurely stroll around Tompkins Square Park to enjoy the fresh air and my latte before returning home to prepare myself a generous brunch with the seasonal produce I had snatched up.

Being the Lighthouse

When I first implemented this, I remember feeling a bit nervous about people's reactions. Much to my surprise, the response was not only positive; it also inspired my friends to do the same. Almost every friend I turned down for a brunch date—or colleague who called me to discuss work—would message me with immense gratitude to express their love for self-care Sundays. Many of them wanted to commit to something similar and were going to block a few hours of their Sundays to do something nice for themselves. I felt empowered by the whole thing: here I was just trying to refill my cup and rejuvenate myself for the week, but it also served a greater purpose of encouraging so many other people in my life to take a stance on their own self-care. You will affect those around you once you start making your well-being a priority. You won't have to preach or explain—being

your bright, energized self and standing strong for your beliefs will inspire those around you to take better care of themselves as well.

I call this "being the lighthouse," and it applies to all the concepts in this book. When you simply take something on and embody it, when you shine your light, people are naturally drawn to you. They become curious about you and ask questions, and that's how you share this whole process with those around you. When we discover new ways to communicate with our bodies, take care of ourselves, and find peace of mind through daily meditation, we want to shout it from the rooftops and share the detailed tutorials with our love ones—I urge you to resist this! You may be jumping up and down with joy and gratitude for this beautiful knowledge, so it's hard not to share it with your loved ones and encourage them to join in.

Every step of the way, I wanted to tell my family everything I was learning. I remember learning about health in elementary school health class and sharing my expertise with parents, but feeling frustrated when they didn't listen to the sagacious wisdom of a six-year-old. This continued when I shifted my eating habits or began my meditation practice—I wanted desperately to teach my family and friends everything I knew, all of these wonderful practices that had changed my life. I realized time and time again it fell on deaf ears.

When I first started practicing Kundalini yoga, I heard one of the teachers talk about "being the lighthouse," and it stuck with me. When we force-feed those around us, in spite of our good intentions, they will resist. However, if we simply stand as the lighthouse and shine as bright as we can, then we lead them to our safe shores where they feel drawn to ask questions. I have seen this work time and time again with people from all walks of life.

I started dating a guy soon after beginning my meditation practice and it reached a point of him spending the night at my place. I panicked when I realized I would miss my evening guided meditation. I had been listening to an Abraham

Hicks guided meditation for releasing negative thoughts and attracting prosperity every day since that dark night, and I had become rather fond of it as part of my nighttime routine. I was torn about breaking my routine for my non-meditating boyfriend. When the time came for us to tuck into bed, I voiced my situation and explained that I always listen to this relaxing guided meditation as I fell asleep. I had no problem putting on earbuds if it bothered him, but if he was interested in hearing it, I could just play it aloud as I normally do. Sure enough, he told me to play it aloud. Not only did he end up telling me the next morning how soothing it was to fall asleep to it, but also he actually made me send it to him so that he could listen on the nights we weren't together. Hilariously enough, he continued listening to that meditation long after we ended our relationship!

That situation turned out so well because at no point was I trying to convince him of the benefits or make a case for him listening to it with me. I simply shared what I was up to and invited him to join or not. It was low pressure, so he was free to open himself without judgment. Similarly, Kenny had known that I was listening to all sorts of guided meditations on YouTube in the evening while I was falling asleep. I knew better than to try to get my brother to meditate, so I never pushed it on him, but he knew I was here if he felt he needed any guidance. One night, a couple of years ago, I got a call from him: "Hey Cass, do you have anything that might help me relax and eventually fall asleep? I haven't been able to get to sleep all week."

> "Don't seek, don't search, don't ask, don't knock, don't demand — relax. If you relax it comes. If you relax, it is there. If you relax, you start vibrating with it." —Osho

And there was my opening because he was coming to me. Not only could I be helpful by providing the tools I had learned and customizing them to his personality, but my words hadn't fallen on deaf ears—because it was him who had come to me. In my personal relationships I do my best not to push anything unless I am invited to give feedback or advice on a particular subject. I focus on the being. Is my presence shining the kind of light I want to share with the world? When my being is a living example of what I preach, I naturally draw in the people who are ready to learn.

Focus your energy on being the lighthouse, lead by example, and attract others who are curious about you so that you can help those who are ready to be helped. When you take care of yourself and fill yourself up all the way, your goodness flows into everything you do and your presence will be far more powerful.

STRESS HURTS

We throw around the "s" word like it's going out of fashion, but the truth is that our bodies were not designed to be this stressed. At the beginning of civilization, the body entered fight-or-flight mode as a response to predators or danger. Today, we turn on our fight-or-flight response as soon as we open our inbox or our calendar. We put our bodies in this perpetual state of stress, and then we wonder why we can't lose weight. We are always exhausted, constantly craving sugar, and experiencing lower fertility rates than ever. News flash—we are doing this to ourselves.

If you are running from a predator for your life, what does your body do? It stores fat, because it doesn't know when you might eat again and it wants to make sure you have fuel to safely get away from danger. It will make you crave sugar (aka fast energy) to keep you going as you're fighting or fleeing. And of course, it's going to decrease your reproductive hormones because it doesn't want to bring a baby into that environment until you are back in safety.

This is why I emphasize the importance of self-care, relaxation, and meditation on your physical being. Shifting your mind from the stressed-out, fight-or-flight response to a calm, peaceful, and centered state will heal your mind and your body.

Laughter Heals. Nature Heals.

Self-care is also about taking care of yourself when you require healing and rejuvenation after emotional trauma, stress, or exhaustion. This essential restoration will make a world of difference in how you feel, look, and operate. But in addition to the self-care I've already discussed, it's important to acknowledge the magical healing power of laughter and nature.

Have you ever laughed so hard that your stomach aches and you begin to cry? Is there anything better? It uplifts our entire being. I find light, contagious laughter—whether it's calling up a girlfriend who always cracks me up, looking up

silly memes on Instagram that get me snorting with laughter, or watching a funny YouTube video—to be one of the most soothing things to fill myself up. Laughing feels good. Joy feels good. It's okay if your jokes are childish, because your transition into laughter is so good for your soul. Hang your adult hat for a few minutes or a few hours and be silly—think of things that are hilarious, and be a total goofball. Cracking yourself up is perfect self-care!

Nature, as you will see in many of the meditations in this book, is a divine healer. I currently live in California, a few blocks away from the ocean, and when work becomes too taxing, I catch a sunrise with my blanket on the sand or take a cycle along the coast and I feel instantly renewed. I will often remove my shoes to feel the sand between my toes and stand before the ocean as restorative therapy and as a reminder of whom I truly am. Even while I was living in Manhattan, I would often lie outside on my blanket in Washington Square Park, surrounded by trees and flowers, and feel grounded and recharged.

I encourage you to take a walk on a tree-lined street, hike up a rocky path, dip your toes in the ocean, or get lost in a forest and connect with the earth. Give all of your hurt, your troubles, and your anxiety over to the earth. Imagine her removing all your ailments. Nature has an amazing power to fill you up and restore you regardless of what you are going through—allow yourself to utilize her.

"BALANCE" IS BULLSH*T

Ah, the word *balance* has us chasing the pot of gold at the end of the rainbow and making up all sorts of #balance. There is something a bit backward in the way a lot of people are using the word *balance* these days. I do not believe in eating kale salads all week and then indulging in donuts all of Friday, and I think we would be better off throwing the word out altogether. If you listen to your intuition and are conscious about the life you are creating, you don't need to balance out the loving actions you do for your body and soul. By consuming foods that genuinely fuel you, you won't need to diet or find "balance."

When you want a glass of wine with dinner, you should enjoy your glass of wine without turning it into an all-out rage with your girlfriends. If your office bestie brings in the best cupcakes in town for her birthday, you should definitely have one, but don't let it derail your day and lead you to a sugar binge. Balance should mean moderation. Enjoy the cupcake, but also enjoy returning to your scheduled programming of foods that nourish your body.

Start your mornings with meditation and have solid rituals in place, which support your best self—these activities keep life in balance during crazy times. Nobody has it all together 100 percent of the time, and I certainly don't. I've met all sorts of highly successful people who are still very much works in progress. When we use our intuition as a compass, balance just happens. Your body will give cues: whether to sit inside and relax or go out on an adventure or dance or hike. Your body will crave different foods if you've been eating the same few vegetables repetitively all month, because it naturally knows how to keep you in balance—we just need to start listening.

You will experience different times in your life when things are crazy, busy, or more topsy-turvy, and it's all part of a much larger balancing act. Don't beat yourself up for it. Ground yourself through turbulent times by using your new skills to challenge your inner guidance. No matter how far you've veered off track, use your inner compass to find your way home.

CHAPTER 5

Integrating Change into Your Daily Life

"You will never change your life until you change something you do daily. The secret of your success is found in your daily routine." —John C. Maxwell

Your life is happening today, right now—not tomorrow, not five years from now. The magic is in this moment. We reflect on our greatest accomplishments such as marriages, promotions, and births, but the majority of our lives are spent between those landmark occasions. We must treat each day like a blank canvas.

By now, you will have discovered new rituals and routines to incorporate into your day-to-day life that will help you reach your ultimate potential. Sometimes we miss the point of the journey because we're so focused on our destination. Addiction programs such as AA often advise of taking things a day at a time, and this can be very useful for many things in life. Sure, it's important to hold grand intentions for your direction, but ground them each day.

If you're working on mindful meal planning and you find it overwhelming, just take it one day at a time. Can you commit to the meals you planned last night and not give in to the urge to snack for just one day? I bet you can! Don't worry about tomorrow; it will be here soon enough. For now, keep your sights on today. Same thing goes for self-care: listening to your body moment-to-moment, in a twenty-four-hour container, and you will find it much more manageable.

Even the worst days only have twenty-four hours. If you are struggling or feeling funky today, it too will pass. In the meantime, do the best you can to be kind to yourself in this moment.

MORNING MEDITATION PRACTICE

Your meditation practice should be taken one day at a time. When my clients first begin their meditation practice, they often ask, "So am I going to have to do this forever?" It cracks me up every time. I then tell them that if they *did* meditate every day, they wouldn't have to ask me that question! Most people who meditate regularly *choose* to do it day after day because of the space, clarity, and calm it gives them. I highly recommend starting a practice and committing to the same meditation for 40 consecutive days. According to yogic science and the Kundalini yoga lineage (that I'm both a teacher and student of), it takes 40 days to fully develop a new habit and or fully release one that's not serving you. I've done this numerous times with different meditations

and new habits in my life and can personally vouch that there is magic in 40. In fact, many of the practices you begin as 40 day-ers end up becoming lifelong rituals that really serve you so you can function at your best.

The Miracle Moment

If you're new to meditation, it helps if you can compare your mind to a Pinterest board. Some of us have fifty to sixty thousand thoughts every day, and out of all of those thoughts, we tend to choose the same 95 percent day after day to "pin" on our mind board. So what does that mean for you? Well, think about an area of your life that you wish were going a little better. You have been pinning those same thoughts and patterns around that area for a very long time. Enter meditation, which I like to say gives us this "miracle moment," where, just like a video game, we see the two options emerge, and we can decide which route we are going to take today. It's that split second where you acknowledge that alternative pin that you haven't been choosing to put on your board for the last few months. That alternative pin will allow you to have that mega shift around a life area in need of repair.

If you've been miserable at work, it can be difficult to see a way out. Instead of focusing on the negatives, find a way to be more positive about the situation. Rather than "there are no fun people here for me to relate to," you might see an alternative such as "there may be more fun people I can relate to." Pin that instead! You are not changing the way you feel, but you are switching your perspective from being resigned to optimistic. More importantly, your energy will be a lot more attractive to fun people at work and may open your eyes to new connections there.

This "miracle moment" applies to every single area of your life. You always have at least two options for how to look at any given situation, and it's the choices you make in those moments that color how you experience your life and how the rest of your life shows up for you! Your morning meditation practice sets you up to navigate the rest of your day with ease, grace, and flow. Your morning practice becomes the foundation in which you can fully blossom into the full beauty you are capable of being. In Kundalini yoga, we call this daily practice *sadhana,* and we do it in the morning before the sun rises, when the world is quiet and our minds are clear. It makes meditation more powerful, and it allows us to have less external noise to battle while doing our practice.

Yogi Bhajan said, *"The greatest reward of doing sadhana is that the person becomes incapable of being defeated. Sadhana is a self-victory, and it is a victory over time and space. Getting up is a victory over time, and doing it is a victory over space. That is what sadhana is."*

I fully experience this for myself. When I wake up at 4 or 5 in the morning and drag myself out of bed, light my candles, do my meditations, and connect within, I feel like superwoman. That's why I laugh when people ask if they have to do this every day. Why would I ever give up that feeling? When I first began meditating, I would go to group *sadhana* at Golden Bridge in NYC. They only had it once a week back then, and I would be so excited to go that I could barely sleep the night before. After grabbing a cab and joining the group downtown, we would all chant and meditate for two and a half hours together, and I would leave around 7 a.m. feeling like there was nothing in the world that I couldn't do. I wanted more of that feeling. In fact, I wanted to start every day feeling like that! So I decided to commit to waking up during *sadhana* hours (between 4 a.m. and 6 a.m.) and lengthening my daily meditation practice.

> *"My daily meditation practice is by far the deepest act of self-love."*

These days, I'm still doing it—and I can still see its ripple effect into my life each and every day. When I tell people what time I wake up and how long I meditate for, they frequently look at me with something like pity in their eyes, and it always gives me a good laugh. My daily meditation practice is by far the deepest act of self-love. It anchors me back to my truth and keeps me calm in the middle of any and every storm this world can and has thrown my way. It is undoubtedly the source of my superpowers. It makes it easier to hear my intuition time and time again amid the noise of the world and people around me. It helps me stay present with my choices each day to make sure they are aligned with my most expansive life, and it helps me show up at a whole new level for all of those I coach or simply interact with every day. My morning is a privilege, and I can't imagine seeing it any other way. I hope you'll join me in using this magnificent tool and let it work wonders in your life, too.

THE NEW YOU

"Shut the door, change the record, clean the house, shake off the dust. Stop being who you were, and change into who you are."
—Paulo Coehlo

Managing other people's opinions can sometimes feel like the biggest burden when making new lifestyle choices. It can be particularly challenging when you are still learning how to navigate your new habits while simultaneously feeling the need to justify your behaviors to others.

You don't need to explain yourself. You get to decide if you want to be open about the journey and with whom to share that information, and it's probably best at the start to limit that to your cheerleaders. If you suspect some people will not encourage you in the journey, I would refrain from sharing too much detail with them. Be the lighthouse. It is much better for them to find out, because they can see that you lost a little weight or that you are glowing with happiness and ask you about it. You will be speaking to open ears that are genuinely interested in what you are up to rather than trying to convert a skeptic.

It's not that people are necessarily closed off or intend to be negative when you tell them about your new habits, how you've started meditating, and listening to your body; it's more likely that it triggers something inside of them because they might be feeling guilty about not doing it themselves. Try not to take it personally because it has absolutely nothing to do with you or your new lifestyle. A person's reaction is simply a reflection of what's going on inside of them. Just as I'm sure you stumbled upon this book at a perfect time for you, when you were truly ready to soak up and

utilize this information, their readiness to make their own shifts will lead them exactly to what they need.

Sometimes you might be the one at fault. If you find yourself apologizing for not having ice cream—because dairy makes you sick—when everyone else has ordered it, you should stop and ask yourself why you feel the need to apologize. What if you knew you would be sent to the hospital after having a little dairy, because you were that allergic to it? I bet you would not feel bad about telling your friends that you can't have ice cream. You would probably express it very matter-of-factly. The more consistent you are with it, the less likely people will even raise an eyebrow at your eating habits. It's a part of who you are now.

Get serious about putting pure fuel into your body. You wouldn't let friends pressure you into drinking a poison that gave you horrible stomach cramps and caused inflammation in your body, right? No way, I know you wouldn't. So if gluten, dairy, or any other food allergy causes a bad reaction—like a terrible stomachache and inflammation—in your body, don't feel bad or guilty for not eating it. My go-to explanation if someone pushes for one is just something simple like, "My body just doesn't digest it properly." I find that a lot of the pushback you get when you try to preach the health benefits of not eating certain foods or eating a certain way, triggers people and makes them feel super self-conscious about their diets. It is never my intention to make someone feel bad about his or her choices. Making the conversation about me and my body's reaction to certain foods keeps it short and sweet, and it gets the point across. And let's be honest, it's exhausting to have to explain the whole thing every single time. Sometimes I just want to eat! Be the lighthouse and allow the people who truly are curious to ask you the deeper questions when they feel called to hear the answer.

CHAPTER 6

Juices and Smoothies

"I am focused on my divine purpose." — Focus Potion   62

"I'm attuned to my magic." — Unicorn Fuel   65

"My beauty radiates from within." — Radiance Juice   67

"I let love be my default setting." — Sunshine Juice   68

"I savor the sweetness in my life." — Blueberry Basil Juice   69

"My discipline is rooted in deep self-love." — Earthy Juice   71

"I choose to fuel myself with pure, clean energy." — Standard Green Machine   72

"I am clear and focused." — Green Lemonade   73

"I allow nature to nourish me." — Farmers' Market Juice   75

"I am well." — Deep-Healing Juice   76

"I am refreshed and relaxed." — Watermelon Mint Juice   78

"My truth is beautiful." — Berry Green Smoothie   79

Focus Potion

Distractions are everywhere these days, especially with smart phones and social media vying for our attention throughout the day. My daily focusing weapon is always my meditation and reciting what I'm here to do. What's your mission statement? I'll give you a hint: For all of us, at its core, it is being a living example of love incarnate. When we adjust our focus through our divine purpose, we have a lot more power when it comes to steering clear of mindless distractions. This potion is a bit of a secret weapon of mine for days when shiny objects are getting the better of me. The sweet combination of grapes with the alkalizing punch of kale and celery perks you up while magical rosemary focuses all that good energy in the area you need it!

DIVINE PURPOSE VISUALIZATION

Sit in easy pose with your eyes closed and focused on your third-eye point (the space between your eyebrows). Take long, deep breaths in through your nose and out your mouth. Feel your body come into a calm balance. Now, bring what your purpose on this planet is to the top of your mind. If you are unclear of what your purpose is, use "I am here to be love," because that is all of our main purpose. Allow it to be your mantra for a few moments, letting it roll around your head, down your spine, and through your breath flow. Now bring to mind what this would look like to you. How do you behave? How do people around you feel and act? What's the ripple effect in the world? Allow these images to flood your mind for the next 3 to 5 minutes before bringing yourself back to your original purpose statement, taking a deep breath in, holding it, and releasing it.

Yield: 1 serving

INGREDIENTS
3 celery stalks
2 cups (134 g) baby kale
1 cup (150 g) grapes
3 drops rosemary essential oil
2 sprigs fresh rosemary, to garnish

1. Put celery, kale, and grapes into a juicer and juice into a large glass.

2. Stir in the rosemary oil, garnish with sprigs of rosemary, and serve immediately.

△ *"I am focused on my divine purpose."*

Unicorn Fuel

One of the major lessons I learned this past year is how important it is to be attuned to my magic. Whenever something in my life feels like it's just "not happening," I take a step back and see how I'm navigating the situation. Am I approaching it as a muggle (for you non–Harry Potter fans out there, this is a non-magical person), or am I approaching it like the magical being I know I am? If I feel stuck, I'm not attuned to my magic. Well, now that you will soon be attuned to your magic, you need to fuel that magical state properly. This smoothie tastes like a piña colada but is powerful (hence the name "unicorn"), delicious, and attractive, yet potent and magical.

KNOW THE FIELD
KUNDALINI MEDITATION

This meditation will help you have a greater experience of your intuitive awareness and therefore help you feel attuned to your magic and trust the flow of energy around you.

Sit in easy pose with your hands in gyan mudra. Close your eyelids nine-tenths of the way, with your eyes looking downward. Concentrate mentally on your third-eye point (the space between your eyebrows). Keeping the spine straight, begin releasing all the tension from the spine, outward. Let each segment of the spine release and each area of the body relax. Continue for 22 minutes, allowing your breath to be natural. It will take about 11 minutes to release your tension. In the second 11-minute cycle, all of your intuitional capacities will be aroused. To close the meditation, take a deep breath in, hold it, and exhale.

Yield: 1 serving

INGREDIENTS
¼ cup (23 g) unsweetened shredded coconut, plus extra to garnish
1 cup (240 ml) unsweetened almond milk
½ cup (83 g) pineapple chunks, plus extra to garnish
1 tablespoon (12 g) raw extra-virgin coconut oil
1 teaspoon cordyceps mushroom powder
1 teaspoon vitamin C powder
1 teaspoon moringa leaf powder

1. Preheat the oven to 350°F (180°C, or gas mark 4). Spread the shredded coconut evenly on a baking sheet and bake for 7–8 minutes, stirring occasionally, until light golden brown.

2. Combine all the ingredients in a blender and purée until thoroughly blended. Fill a large glass with ice, add the juice, and garnish with pineapple chunks and toasted coconut, if desired. Serve immediately.

 "I'm attuned to my magic."

Radiance Juice

Roald Dahl famously said: "If you have good thoughts, they will shine out of your face like sunbeams and you will always look lovely." I couldn't agree more. Beauty starts from within and permeates outward. Thinking thoughts that nourish your soul and eating foods that nourish your body are more effective than the most luxurious makeup money can buy. You can't fake true radiance. This juice is packed with nutrients that will get you glowing from the inside out! Pineapple juice promotes healthy skin and helps prevent acne; watercress is also great for your overall health with its high levels of vitamin C; and cucumber has cooling and moisturizing properties.

RADIANT HEART MEDITATION

In this exercise, we are going to pull energy into our heart center and allow it to saturate every cell of our being, filling us with light and allowing our inner radiance to pour outward as it overflows.

Begin by sitting in easy pose and breathing long and deep. Close your eyes and focus on your heart center while using your hands to slowly and steadily pull the energy surrounding you into your heart. Your hands should stay at heart height and move from the sides of your body inward, as if you are catching a ball and bringing it into your heart. Feel the light in your heart expand and grow brighter with each motion. Continue for at least 3 minutes, gradually building up to 11 minutes. Take a deep breath in and bring your hands into your heart, right palm on top of left. Feel the energy pulsing through your heart center and allow it to distribute throughout your entire being. Imagine it filling up each cell with its loving light energy. Exhale.

Yield: 1 serving

INGREDIENTS
½ cup (17 g) watercress
2 cucumbers, peeled
2 limes, peeled
1 cup (166 g) pineapple chunks

1. Starting with the watercress, juice all the ingredients into a large glass.

2. Lightly stir and serve immediately.

"My beauty radiates from within."

Sunshine Juice

When something vexing comes up in your day, ask yourself, "What would I do if love was my default setting?" So when that guy cuts you off on the way to work, blast him with love, knowing that he must have been in a bad place to drive so irresponsibly. When we choose love, everything feels a whole lot lighter! I originally created this juice to disguise the taste of carrot juice, which I don't like. To my surprise, it ended up tasting so good and being such a natural pick-me-up that I nicknamed it my "sunshine juice," because I literally feel like I'm beaming rays of sunshine after I drink it.

CHOOSING LOVE MEDITATION

Sit in easy pose. Close your eyes and place your hands at your heart center, right on top of left. Take long, deep breaths through your nose and out your mouth, feeling the energy in your heart center expand with each breath. Allow any thoughts that have been weighing on you or situations you have been struggling with to float into your mind, one at a time. After seeing the thought, mentally say to yourself, "I could choose love instead of this." Sometimes, the loving solution may pop into your head just as you silently make the declaration; other times, it may be less apparent. Regardless, continue through your grievance inventory for 3 to 5 minutes, mentally saying "I could choose love instead of this" after each thought. When your time is up or you have made it through your list and feel at peace, take a deep breath in, hold it, and allow "I let love be my default setting" saturate your being for the next 10 to 15 seconds. Exhale.

Yield: 1 serving

INGREDIENTS
5 carrots
3 oranges, peeled and quartered
1 grapefruit, peeled and quartered
1 apple, coarsely chopped
1 lemon, peeled

1. Juice all the ingredients into a large glass.

2. Lightly stir and serve immediately.

△ "I let love be my default setting."

Blueberry Basil Juice

Think of a situation that is causing you stress or making you upset. Now think about all the blessings you have in your life at the moment. Maybe it's a comfy bed or a healthy body, a sunny day or a beautiful plate of food to eat. When we shift our attention from the "perceived problem" that is the cause of the stress to the sweetness all around us in each moment, we see things with greater clarity, allowing us to revel in our blissful, blessed lives! Drink this juice and soak up the sweetness of clarity in your life and open up the portal for a clearer mind, body, and soul.

SWEET MOMENTS MEDITATION

This meditation is a little different because it involves a series of little moments throughout the day. The intention of this meditation is to get you into the practice of "savoring the sweetness" in your day-to-day life. Set hourly alarms on your phone for the day with the message "take a sweet moment" or "savor the sweetness" on each alert. As each alarm sounds, stop what you're doing and give yourself a full minute to take some deep breaths and recalibrate your mind to the sweetness of that moment. Allow yourself to be inspired by the first thing that pops into your mind, to be grateful for it, and to let that feeling permeate your being while the breath calms and centers you. Repeat as many times as necessary with the intention of integrating it into your every day.

Yield: 1 serving

INGREDIENTS

5 sprigs basil
2 cups (134 g) chopped kale
1 green apple, coarsely chopped
1 lemon, peeled
1 cup (150 g) blueberries
¼ cup (36 g) blackberries

1. Starting with the basil, juice all the ingredients into a large glass.

2. Lightly stir and serve immediately.

△ *"I savor the sweetness in my life."*

Earthy Juice

For a while there, I despised discipline. But I've learned that discipline can be your greatest super-power when it comes from a place of self-love. I'm committed to my daily meditation practice, to nourishing my body with foods that truly fuel it, and to listening to my inner-guidance system. Does this mean there aren't days when I don't want to drag myself out of bed to meditate at the crack of dawn? Of course not! But, when I remind myself of what's for my highest good, I get back to what truly supports me. This juice will connect you back to the rooted energy of the earth. The rich beet and carrots will increase your connection with your natural strength and discipline while the parsley and lemon will detoxify anything in your system that might be getting in your way.

CALIBER OF LIFE
KUNDALINI MEDITATION

This meditation is known to help manage normal depression and discouragement and increase the caliber for excellence in your life.

Sit in easy pose. Extend both arms straight forward and parallel to the ground. Curl the fingers of your right hand into a fist and extend your thumb straight up. Keep your elbow straight and move the fist to the center of your body. Move your left arm to the center and wrap the fingers of your left hand around the outside of the right hand's fist. Extend your left thumb straight up. Adjust the grip of the hands so that the thumbs can touch along their sides as they point up and the tips of the thumbs form a little V. Focus the eyes on the thumbnails and through the V. Inhale deeply and fill the lungs for 5 seconds. Exhale completely and empty the lungs for 5 seconds. Then hold the breath out as you stay still for 15 seconds. Continue this breathing for 3 minutes to begin, gradually building up to 11 minutes. End the meditation with a deep breath in, hold it, and exhale.

Yield: 1 Serving

INGREDIENTS
3 sprigs parsley
2 carrots
1 beet, peeled
1 red apple, coarsely chopped
1 lemon, peeled

1. Starting with the parsley, juice all the ingredients into a large glass.

2. Lightly stir and serve immediately.

"My discipline is rooted in deep self-love."

Standard Green Machine

We have a choice each day about how we want to feel, how clear we want to think, and how easily we want to connect with that loving voice inside that's always guiding us toward our best interests. Your fuel decides your focus. When we treat our body to nurturing foods, particularly alkalizing greens, we turn down our mind's inner static, our energy level rises, and we get back into our "groove." If you have been feeling foggy, check your fuel. Make "going for the greens" your default and you will welcome a completely new level of functioning. This juice is loaded with alkalizing vegetables to help cure that brain fog and give you the jolt you need to get through the day.

EGO ERADICATOR

This activating Kundalini meditation helps energize your system and clear your head—a potent one-two punch when combined with a morning green juice, and a great substitute for your afternoon coffee!

Sit in easy pose with your hands in prayer position at your heart's center. Tune in with the adi mantra "ong-namo-guru-dev-namo" three times. Then raise your arms to 60 degrees, touch your fingers to the pads of your palms (as if you're filing your nails) and stick your thumbs up (imagine you are plugging your thumbs into the ceiling). Now begin sharply exhaling and inhaling out of your mouth, focusing on the exhale (imagine you are blowing out a candle with your nose, then allow the inhale to naturally match it). Keep this breath going, with your elbows straight and thumbs plugged in, for 1 minute to begin with, gradually building up to 11 minutes. When time is up, take in a deep breath and keep your hands up, allowing your thumbs to move toward each other until they are touching. Release your fingers and exhale after 10 seconds. Allow your hands to float down to the sides of your body and touch the floor. Sit and enjoy the crystal-clear energy flowing throughout your system.

Yield: 1 serving

INGREDIENTS
3 celery stalks
1 green apple, coarsely chopped
½ cucumber, peeled
½ lemon, peeled
3 cups (90 g) spinach
2 cups (134 g) chopped kale
2-inch (5 cm) piece ginger root

1. Juice all the ingredients into a large glass.

2. Lightly stir and serve immediately.

"I choose to fuel myself with pure, clean energy."

Green Lemonade

I used to get easily distracted, with sugar and caffeine majorly contributing to my "distraction disorder." So I replaced sugar and caffeine with a powerful, alkalizing daily green juice and a *pranayam* (breath work practice), which turned out to be the best cure for getting back my beautiful clarity and focus!

PRANAYAM ENERGIZER SERIES

Breath of Fire. Sit in easy pose and place your hands in gyan mudra. Begin rapid and forceful breathing out your nose (as if you were blowing out a candle with your nose). Focus on the exhale and allow the inhale to come reflexively. Continue breathing for 3½ minutes, then inhale deeply and hold the breath for 10 seconds. Exhale and relax

Long Deep Breathing. In the same pose, breathe in long, complete, yogic breaths. Breathe deeper than normal so that your entire rib cage is used and lifts several inches on the inhale. Exhale and pull your navel all the way back. Consciously follow each part of the breath. Continue for 2½ minutes, then inhale and hold for 10 seconds. Exhale and relax.

Pucker your lips and immediately inhale deeply through them. Exhale through the nose. Continue for 90 seconds, then inhale, hold briefly, and exhale.

Breath of Fire. Repeat exercise 1. Make your breathing powerful and regular for 1 minute, then inhale deeply and hold, as you focus on your third-eye point (the space between your eyebrows). Exhale and relax.

Breath Awareness. Meditate on the flow of breath as you relax and your breath settles into a normal rhythm. Feel the subtle pathways of the breath throughout your body. Sense the breath as a motion and experience the different kinds of energy that flow into every organ and cell.

Yield: 1 serving

INGREDIENTS
5 romaine lettuce leaves
3 lemons, peeled
1 cucumber, peeled
1 pear, coarsely chopped
1 cup (68 g) chopped kale

1. Juice all the ingredients into a large glass.

2. Lightly stir and serve immediately.

"I am clear and focused."

Farmers' Market Juice

When you are feeling drained, I urge you to let nature nourish and recharge you. It can be as simple as eating your lunch under a tree on a blanket, or tossing off your shoes and relishing in the beautiful grounded feeling of your feet on the earth. This juice is packed with a variety of nutrients from some of my go-to veggies, along with ginger and parsley. I encourage you to experiment with the ingredients depending on what's seasonally available at your local farmers' market.

WALK IN NATURE MEDITATION

Okay, I'm making you get outside for this one! Go to a local garden, park, beach, or even just a path with a lot of trees nearby. If you feel comfortable, take off your shoes and walk barefoot; if not, just imagine that your feet are connected with the ground with each step you take. Turn off your cell phone and put it away. Spend anywhere from 5 to 20 minutes focusing on your breath and taking in the beauty around you. You can also add a silent mantra if you'd like: simply say to yourself "sat" on the inhale and "nam" on the exhale with every step you take. This is a Kundalini mantra that means true self—personally, it grounds me and brings me back to the truth of who I am when I meditate on it.

Yield: 1 serving

INGREDIENTS
½ cup (30 g) parsley
8 romaine lettuce leaves
4 carrots
2 apples, coarsely chopped
2 cups (60 g) spinach
1-inch (2.5 cm) piece ginger root

1. Starting with the parsley, juice all the ingredients into a large glass.

2. Lightly stir and serve immediately.

△ *"I allow nature to nourish me."*

Deep-Healing Juice

Isn't it funny how we take feeling healthy for granted? Most of us don't even think about how good it feels to be up and functioning on a day-to-day basis until a malady of some sort creeps in and renders us useless. So whether this meditation and recipe find you in perfect health or feeling a bit out of sorts, let this be a reminder that taking care of yourself, getting the rest and nourishment that your body is craving, and sitting in gratitude for your beautiful working body is an ever-present lesson for all of us. This powerful tonic is my secret to getting back on my feet in no time when I'm feeling under the weather. Along with the usual healing suspects, such as ginger and turmeric, I've added my secret weapon, oregano oil.

HEALING LIGHT MEDITATION

You may want to take a short nap following this meditation and let it all soak in, if your schedule allows.

Cover a bed, couch, or yoga mat with a soft blanket and lie down on your back. Close your eyes and turn your focus to your breath, deeply breathing in through your nose and out your mouth. Allow your breath to circulate throughout your body, feeling it in every nook and cranny and clearing it out on your exhale, releasing toxins out of your body. Repeat this for several breaths and then visualize a bright green light and welcome it in. Feel this light penetrate every part of your body, especially those areas that need healing—envision it infiltrating every cell in those areas and restoring them to health. If you connect to a particular divine figure, feel free to bring them in to help guide this light. When you are ready, take a deep breath in and hold it, allowing the green light to flood your entire system and soak up any toxic impurities, then exhale powerfully and release them out of your system.

Yield: 1 serving

INGREDIENTS

3 oranges, peeled and quartered

1 grapefruit, peeled and quartered

2-inch (5 cm) piece ginger root

2-inch (5 cm) piece turmeric root

2 to 4 drops oregano essential oil (this oil can be potent, so I recommend starting out with a small amount)

1. Juice all the ingredients into a large glass.

2. Add the oregano oil, stir well, and serve immediately.

△ *"I am well."*

Watermelon Mint Juice

Do you often find yourself pining for a vacation? Well, this cooling meditation combined with my delicious and refreshing watermelon mint juice is my insta-vacay and it's way more cost-effective. We have control over our state of being at every point of the day, so if there's a fire-filled stress pit in the atmosphere of your personal universe, I am happy to let you know that you can also call in a breeze and peaceful rainfall to cool down and refresh your inner landscape. This juice is always a special treat for me and feels like a rejuvenating island breeze at just the right time of the day. I love the balance of the watermelon with the cooling, alkalizing cucumber and refreshing mint.

SITALI PRANAYAM (COOLING BREATH)

Sit in easy pose and place your hands in gyan mudra. Stick your tongue out and curl it up like you are forming a taco-shell shape. If you can't curl your tongue, simply keep your tongue out and make an "O" shape with your mouth so that it naturally bends. Breathe in deeply through your tongue and mouth, allowing the air to fill you all the way up, then release through your nose. Repeat for 3 minutes, focusing on your breath and allowing yourself to enjoy the cooling sensation. To close, take a deep breath in, hold, and release. This breath will leave you feeling cool, calm, and refreshed, and is a great daily practice.

Yield: 1 serving

INGREDIENTS
1 cucumber, peeled
1¼ cups (190 g) chopped watermelon
½ cup (15 g) fresh mint leaves
3 drops lavender essential oil (optional)

1. Juice all the ingredients into a large glass.

2. Lightly stir, add the lavender essential oil, if using, and serve immediately.

△ *"I am refreshed and relaxed."*

Berry Green Smoothie

The truth of who you are is beautiful and when you fully love and accept it—imperfections and all—you give others around you permission to love and accept themselves. This smoothie is a perfect companion to loving and accepting your truth. It has good-for-you greens, antioxidant-packed berries, and a sweet creaminess from the banana and almond butter. I like to add reishi for an additional immune system boost.

CONQUER SELF-ANIMOSITY KUNDALINI MEDITATION

Self-defeating activity and self-animosity occur when we do not accept ourselves. This meditation conquers such a state and gives you the ability for constant consciousness in support of the core self.

Sit in easy pose with an alert attitude. Relax your arms at your sides and raise your forearms up and in, toward your chest at heart level. Draw your hands into fists and point your thumbs straight up to the sky. Press your fists together in such a manner that your thumbs and fists are touching—the palms are toward each other. This meditation requires the upper torso to be held straight, without rocking back and forth. Fix your eyes at the tip of your nose. Inhale through your nose and exhale out your mouth, and then inhale through your mouth and exhale through your nose. Continue for 3 minutes, gradually building up to 11 minutes. End the meditation by taking a big inhale and stretching your arms up over your head. Keep this position while you take three more deep breaths and then relax.

Yield: 1 serving

INGREDIENTS
1 banana
1 cup (240 ml) unsweetened almond milk
½ cup (93 g) frozen mixed berries
½ cup (34 g) chopped kale
1 tablespoon (16 g) cashew or almond butter
1 heaping teaspoon reishi mushroom powder (optional)

1. Combine all the ingredients in a blender and purée until thoroughly blended.

2. Pour into a large glass and serve immediately.

"My truth is beautiful."

CHAPTER 7
Breakfast

"I am rigged for success." — Avocado Toast Three Ways 82

"I choose to do things I love." — Pumpkin Quinoa Pancakes 85

"I enjoy the ease and flow of life." — AB&J Rice Cakes 87

"My life is a reflection of how sweet I am to myself." — Chia Seed Pudding 88

"I am full within myself." — Avocado Black Bean Hash 90

"I allow myself the space to think before deciding." — Quinoa Porridge 91

"I release my expectations." — Creamy Cashew Yogurt 93

"I honor my basic needs." — Veggie Scramble with Turmeric Potatoes 95

"I am grounded in possibility." — Chilled Oatmeal 97

"I honor what's working." — Blueberry Almond Muffins 98

"I embrace my quirks with love." — Cherry Rosemary Scones 101

"I appreciate my abundance." — Brunch Tacos 102

"I am ready to take a leap of faith." — Chia Seed Pancakes 105

"I am taking care of myself." — Crack Bars 107

"I am loved and supported." — Strawberry-Banana Gluten-Free Cakes 109

Avocado Toast Three Ways

We can't be well-oiled machines all of the time; our lives can get messy or chaotic, which is why I think it's so important to know ourselves and prepare accordingly. For example, if you are tempted to stay up working all night and neglect your self-care, set your phone alarm to go off at 9 p.m. to remind you to close your laptop and enjoy a bath. Avocado toast is one of those meals that has helped rig a lot of people for success around their diets. It's a super easy, filling, go-to, healthy breakfast or lunch. Here are three of my favorite recipes, but I encourage you to explore your own creativity here.

INNER ROCK STAR VISUALIZATION

Sit comfortably with your spine straight and your eyes closed. Imagine yourself going through the day ahead as your best self: you are sailing through the same meetings, tasks, errands, and interactions with ease, grace, confidence, and bliss. Go through your day thoroughly and all the activities involved and notice the energy that this "rock star you" brings to each situation. When you've gone through your whole day, take a deep breath in and hold it, allowing all of that magnificent energy to circulate within your body, then exhale.

Yield: 1 serving (per option)

INGREDIENTS

OPTION 1

2 tablespoons (30 g) roasted garlic hummus
1 slice Ezekiel bread, toasted
1 avocado, halved, pitted, and sliced
    cup (34 g) sautéed kale (see page 104)
    cup (44 g) sautéed red onions
Pinch of salt
Pinch of freshly ground black pepper

OPTION 2

1 avocado, halved, pitted, and mashed
1 flatbread cracker (I love the seasoned ones
    from Wasa)
1 radish, thinly sliced
Spring peas, cooked
Drizzle of extra-virgin olive oil
Pinch of salt

OPTION 3

1 avocado, halved, pitted, and mashed
1 brown rice cake
1 fresh peach, sliced and sautéed in extra-virgin
    coconut oil

To make option 1, spread the hummus on the bread. Top with the sliced avocado, sautéed kale, and red onions, and season with a pinch of salt and pepper. Serve.

To make option 2, spread the mashed avocado on the flatbread. Arrange the sliced radish on top and scatter over the peas. Drizzle over the olive oil and season with salt. Serve.

To make option 3, spread the mashed avocado on the rice cake, then top with the peach slices. Serve.

"I am rigged for success."

Pumpkin Quinoa Pancakes

Life can drag you in a million different directions each day, but you can stop the treadmill of insanity whenever you take a moment, connect to your breath, and choose to do what you love—what your soul wants and what ultimately is for your highest good. Our life expands when we start choosing to do things we love with the time and energy we have.

MEDITATION FOR THE POSITIVE MIND

Sit in easy pose. Curl your ring finger and little finger into each palm with your thumbs holding them down, with your two standing fingers held together instead of spread apart as in a peace sign. Bring in your arms so that your elbows are by your sides and your hands are by your shoulders with the two standing fingers of each hand pointing straight up. Your forearms and hands should tilt forward slightly to an angle of 30 degrees from the vertical. Press your shoulders and elbows back firmly but comfortably and keep your palms facing forward. Close your eyes and focus them on your third-eye point (the space between your eyebrows). Take slow deep breaths and mentally chant "sa ta na ma" from the third-eye point outward. This is a common Kundalini mantra that describes the cycle of life: "sa" means infinity, "ta" is life, "na" is death, and "ma" is rebirth. Start by practicing for 11 minutes, gradually building up to 31 minutes. Take a deep breath in to close, hold it, and then exhale and relax.

Yield: 2 servings

INGREDIENTS

½ cup (120 ml) unsweetened almond milk

1 teaspoon cream of tartar

2 teaspoons flaxseed meal

2 tablespoons (30 ml) water

1 cup (112 g) quinoa flour

½ cup (123 g) pumpkin purée

2 tablespoons (30 ml) pumpkin pie spice (for homemade pumpkin pie spice, mix ½ teaspoon ground cinnamon, ⅛ teaspoon ground cloves, ¼ teaspoon ground ginger, and ⅛ teaspoon ground nutmeg)

2 tablespoons (30 ml) extra-virgin coconut oil

1 tablespoon (15 ml) vanilla extract

Coconut oil cooking spray, for greasing

FILLING (OPTIONAL)

8-ounce (237 g) container vegan cream cheese

2 tablespoons (30 ml) date syrup

Sprinkle of ground nutmeg and cinnamon

Dash of vanilla extract

(continued on page 86)

"I choose to do things I love."

1. In a small cup, combine the almond milk and cream of tartar and set aside.

2. To make flax "egg," mix together the flaxseed and water in a small bowl and set aside for 5 minutes, until thickened.

3. In a medium mixing bowl, mix together the quinoa flour, pumpkin purée, pumpkin pie spice, coconut oil, vanilla extract, and the flax "egg."

4. Spray a medium frying pan or griddle pan with the cooking spray and heat over medium heat. Add the almond milk mixture to the mixing bowl and thoroughly mix. Pour 2 tablespoons of the mixture into the pan and cook for 3 to 5 minutes, or until bubbles start to form and the edges begin to crisp. Flip and cook for another 30 seconds, and then transfer to a serving plate. Repeat with the remaining mixture.

5. To make the filling, if using, combine all the filling ingredients in a stand mixer and beat until smooth and creamy. To serve, I love making silver dollar pancakes and stacking them with layers of the filling in between.

AB&J Rice Cakes

LET. IT. BE. EASY. Those four words have been a major game changer for me. We have a choice to let it be easy. Does it mean that sometimes you're still going to have to take action and get things done? Sure, but you can either choose to do it with ease and flow or fight tooth and nail. What are you making "hard" or "difficult" in your life? Maybe it's dating, starting a business, or losing weight. How much energy are you putting into your story about how hard it is? You can reprogram your mind to actually LET IT BE EASY. Like going to the gym, you are going to have to do some reps here—the first one hundred times, your mind is going to want to go back to your familiar story of struggle. However, over time, you will shift it through your conscious effort and create the new, improved story of just how easy that area of your life flows. This recipe is a simple yet nourishing breakfast in a pinch. It's okay. Go ahead and let it be easy for you!

WAVES OF ABUNDANCE MEDITATION

This is a little personal practice of mine that I do at any time throughout the day in any position, especially when I feel the need to get back into the natural ease and flow of my life. I'll take a little time, even if it's while sitting on a park bench or running errands, and put on an uplifting song.

Close your eyes and imagine yourself standing in the middle of the ocean with beautiful, big waves gently rolling toward you. Allow yourself to sit in this powerful, natural flow of water and feel all of the blessings on their way. After a few moments, envision yourself leaning back into the water and supporting you as you float and soak in the rays of the sun. Allow this feeling to bring you back to your truth and remind you to enjoy the ease and flow of life.

Yield: 1 serving

INGREDIENTS

2 tablespoons (32 g) almond butter (or nut butter of your choice)
2 brown rice cakes
½ cup (83 g) sliced strawberries (or bananas or blueberries)
Sprinkle of ground cinnamon

1. Spread a tablespoon of almond butter on each rice cake.

2. Top with the sliced strawberries and a sprinkle of cinnamon, and serve.

"I enjoy the ease and flow of life."

Chia Seed Pudding

Often when we are craving sweetness, especially first thing in the morning, it comes from a deep need to treat ourselves more "sweetly." If you find yourself reaching for the sugar or something else that gives you relaxation or pleasure, it's time to take a look in the mirror. Do you really want that ice cream, or do you just need a break and want to relax? This pudding was a very helpful breakfast, snack, and dessert for me when I was first transitioning off sugar. The vanilla, cinnamon, and berries in this pudding are all truly nourishing ways to quiet that sweet craving.

SELF-LOVE MEDITATION

Light one or two of your favorite candles, put on a love song you adore, and sit in easy pose in a cozy spot in your home. Place your hands over your heart center, right on top of left. Feel the warmth and pulse of your heart as you close your eyes and take long, deep breaths. Feel a bright ball of golden light at your heart center, growing with each breath and creeping into every nook and cranny of your being. Allow yourself to enjoy this connection with the love you have within. Feel yourself being held by your own loving energy as you would feel being held by a romantic partner. Stimulate that feeling from within and allow yourself to marinate in your own warm, loving light. When you are ready to release, take a deep breath in and hold it, allowing the light from your heart to seep through every particle of your being and form a big "love bubble" around you. Hold for 15 seconds and then exhale, slowly bringing yourself back into the room.

Yield: 1 serving

INGREDIENTS

1 cup (238 ml) unsweetened vanilla coconut milk
⅓ cup (40 g) chia seeds
½ teaspoon vanilla extract
Pinch of ground cinnamon
Pinch of ground nutmeg
Pinch of ground cardamom
Fresh berries, to serve
Nuts, to serve

1. In a mason jar or a small bowl, combine the coconut milk with the chia seeds. Add in your cinnamon, nutmeg, and cardamom. Mix and let sit in the refrigerator for an hour or until it reaches a pudding-like consistency. Stir periodically, if needed, to evenly distribute the chia seeds.

2. To serve, top with berries and nuts.

"My life is a reflection of how sweet I am to myself."

Avocado Black Bean Hash

Often when we reach for more filling comfort foods, it's because we don't feel full within ourselves. Take some time today to observe the ways you reach outside of yourself to feel full. What would it feel like to rewire those patterns so that you reached inward to fill your cup? A nice hearty breakfast gives me the energy to move through my day feeling grounded and supported in my body, and this hash can be thrown together quickly.

LIGHT-FILLED MEDITATION

Sit in easy pose with your palms facing up. Start taking long, deep breaths in through your nose and out your mouth. Visualize a golden ball of light at the center of your being, and with each inhale, see that golden light expand and grow brighter. Keep breathing as the light keeps expanding and begins to fill up your entire being with golden light. Allow that light to keep expanding beyond your body and surround you in a golden ball of light. Take this energy in, and feel how supported and held you are from your inner light source. Continue for 3 minutes, then take a deep breath in, hold it, and allow the golden light to saturate every cell of your being. Exhale and relax.

Yield: 2 to 4 servings

INGREDIENTS

3 tablespoons (45 ml) olive oil, divided

6 small fingerling (or new) potatoes, sliced into ¼-inch (6 mm) thick rounds

Salt and freshly ground black pepper, to taste

1 red onion, diced

2 avocados, halved and pitted, divided

1 green pepper, seeded and chopped

1 cup (172 g) precooked black beans, drained and rinsed

1 cup (150 g) cherry tomatoes, halved

½ cup (82 g) corn kernels

1. Preheat the oven to 425°F (220°C, or gas mark 7). Use 1 tablespoon (15 ml) olive oil to lightly grease a medium baking sheet. Spread out the potatoes and lightly season with salt and pepper. Roast in the oven for 5 minutes, or until the edges start to brown.

2. In the meantime, heat the remaining 2 tablespoons (30 ml) oil in a large frying pan over medium heat. Sauté the onion for 3 to 4 minutes, or until it starts to brown. Chop one of the avocados, stir it into the pan, and then add the green pepper, black beans, tomatoes, and corn. Reduce the heat to low and check on the potatoes. Add the potatoes to the pan and increase the heat to medium.

3. Mix for another 1 to 2 minutes, and then transfer to a serving dish. Slice the remaining avocado, add to the dish, and serve.

"I am full within myself."

Quinoa Porridge

I like to refer to those few seconds when we have to decide how we want to react to something as the "miracle moment." Sure, it's a good idea "to sleep on it," or in my case, meditate on the bigger decision at hand, but sometimes we're put in a situation where we have to quickly decide how we are going to react, and that may have a tremendous impact on our lives. When we anchor ourselves in a daily meditation practice, we give ourselves the space—that miracle moment—to see the options in front of us. Once we allow ourselves the space to think before we decide how to act, we step into our power around our responses. This warm, nourishing porridge feels like oatmeal but is loaded with a lot more protein thanks to our friend quinoa. It's the perfect way to ground yourself before a hectic day.

STILL THE MIND
KUNDALINI MEDITATION

Sit in easy pose with your shoulders relaxed, and your palms facing up and gently resting on your knees. Close your eyes and focus on the tip of your nose. Breathe in and out normally through the nose; open your mouth as wide as possible and stick your tongue on your upper palate. Hold this position for 3 minutes while breathing through your nose. Take a deep breath in, hold it, and exhale to close.

Yield: 1 serving

INGREDIENTS
1 cup (185 g) cooked quinoa

1 cup (238 ml) unsweetened vanilla coconut milk

1 peach (or any seasonal fruit), cut into small chunks

½ banana, sliced

3 tablespoons (27 g) chia seeds

¼ cup (18 g) sliced almonds (or nut/seed of your choice)

¼ cup (40 g) hemp hearts

1. In a small saucepan, combine the quinoa, coconut milk, and a little more than half of the peaches and banana and heat over medium-low heat. Add the chia seeds and stir continuously for 4 to 5 minutes, or until the mixture thickens and almost reaches a boil. Remove from the heat and set aside.

2. Transfer the quinoa porridge to a bowl, add the sliced almonds, hemp hearts, and remaining fruit, and then serve!

"I allow myself the space to think before deciding."

Creamy Cashew Yogurt

When we release our expectations and let go of expecting certain outcomes, we can accept that sometimes we do not know what's best for us. Take a step back and let go of what you think is best. It's okay to hold the space for your goals and aspirations, but hold them lightly and show up for what's happening in front of you. Whatever is happening in your life, it's happening *for* you, not *to* you, so take your power back, release those expectations, and empower yourself to make the best of what is. When I first started toying around with making an alternative "yogurt," I had no idea how it would turn out. But I soon discovered that cashews make a perfect dairy-free Greek-esque yogurt. Keep a big batch in the fridge and toss some berries and granola in as you move through your week.

LET GO MEDITATION

Sit in a comfortable position, place your palms facing up on your knees, and start breathing in through your nose and out your mouth. Allow your attention to focus on your breath and add the mantra "let go," breathing in "let" and exhaling "go." When other thoughts come up, let them float by like clouds and keep coming back to your breathing and the "let go" mantra. Continue for 3 minutes, gradually building up to 20 minutes. To close the meditation, take a deep breath in, hold it, and exhale powerfully.

Yield: 6 servings

INGREDIENTS
1½ cups (195 g) raw unsalted cashew nuts
Juice of 1 lemon
⅓ cup (80 ml) canned coconut milk
1 tablespoon (15 ml) vanilla extract
Raspberries, to serve (optional)

1. In a bowl, combine the cashew nuts and enough cold water to cover and soak for 2 to 3 hours. Drain.

2. Combine all the ingredients in a food processor or blender and purée until the mixture has a yogurt-like consistency.

3. Garnish with raspberries, if desired, and serve.

△ "I release my expectations."

Veggie Scramble with Turmeric Potatoes

When we take care of ourselves, we create a momentum that allows the universe to take care of us as well. When your needs are met, you are able to help other people at a higher level, make decisions for the greater good, and make a positive impact on everyone you come in contact with that day. This veggie scramble quickly became one of my go-to breakfasts once I started a plant-based diet and still wanted the "feel" and heartiness of my old scrambled eggs with potatoes.

MEDITATION FOR INCREASED ENERGY

Sit comfortably with your spine straight. Place your palms together in prayer pose at the center of the chest with the fingers pointing up. Focus on your third-eye point (the space between your eyebrows), and up a bit, at the root of your nose. This is the location of the sixth chakra, the command center of both your subtle intuition and your glandular system.

As you inhale, divide the breath into four equal sniffs. Hold in a few seconds. Exhale as well in four equal segments. Hold out a few seconds. On each sniff of the inhale and exhale, pull your navel toward your spine. One full breath cycle should take about 7 to 8 seconds. If your mind is anxious or your thoughts are distracting you, add the mantra "sa ta na ma" on both the inhale and exhale. "Sa" is infinity, "ta" is life, "na" is death, and "ma" is rebirth. This mantra will help focus your mind, and the power of the vibration of "Sa Ta Na Ma" stimulates connection with the true self. Continue for 3 to 5 minutes. Bring the meditation to a close by inhaling deeply and pressing your palms together with maximum force for 10 seconds. Relax for 15 to 30 seconds. Repeat this ending two more times. Relax.

Yield: 2 servings

INGREDIENTS

5 small fingerling (or new) potatoes, sliced into ¼-inch (6 mm) thick rounds
2 tablespoons (30 ml) olive oil, divided
1 teaspoon ground turmeric
1 teaspoon garlic powder
1 teaspoon onion powder
1 teaspoon dried oregano
1 white onion, diced
1 clove to 1 bulb garlic, cloves separated, peeled, and chopped (amount depends on your taste)
½ zucchini, sliced
2 cups (220 g) leafy greens (I like a blend of baby kale, spinach, and bok choy)
½ cup (32 g) enoki mushrooms
½ avocado, halved, pitted, and sliced

(continued on page 96)

"I honor my basic needs."

1. Preheat your oven to 425°F (220°C, or gas mark 7).

2. In a small bowl, combine the potatoes, 1 tablespoon (15 ml) olive oil, turmeric, garlic powder, onion powder, and oregano and toss well. Pour the potatoes onto a baking sheet and roast for 10 minutes.

3. Meanwhile, heat the remaining 1 tablespoon (15 ml) olive oil in a medium frying pan over medium heat. Add the onion and garlic, stir for 1 to 2 minutes, and then add the zucchini. Cook for another 5 minutes, until golden and tender. Add the leafy greens and continue to stir until the greens are bright green and wilted. Transfer the mixture to a serving plate.

4. Check on the potatoes and if they have started to brown, remove them from the oven and let them cool on the stove top. If they still have a few minutes to go, leave them in while you finish up the last few steps.

5. In the same frying pan (no need to clean), heat the mushrooms over medium heat and fry until browned. Place the mushrooms on top of the vegetable mixture. Serve the roasted potatoes on the side and top it all off with sliced avocado!

Chilled Oatmeal

As I was writing this recipe, I was in a bit of a funk. A relationship I cared about was ending, and in my head, I was focusing on the loss of possibility. I realized that when we feel as if our options are diminishing rather than expanding, we can't help but feel distressed. When we sit from a place of trust and turn our vision to the incredible amount of possibilities before us, we naturally shift into a place of ease, flow, and peace. Oatmeal is a grounding treat that can put us in a calm state to see the possibilities ahead.

MEDITATION FOR BALANCING THE NERVOUS ENERGIES

Sit in easy pose. With your elbows out, connect your hands a few inches in front of your heart center, palms facing the chest. Place the palm of your right hand against the back of your left hand. Keep your hands and forearms parallel to the ground so that the fingers of the right hand point toward the left side and the fingers of the left hand point toward the right side. Press your thumb tips together. Close your eyes almost all the way, leaving just a slit of light coming through. Inhale deeply through your nose and hold the breath in for 15 to 20 seconds, then exhale through the nose and hold the breath out for 15 to 20 seconds. Continue for 3 minutes. To close the meditation, take a deep breath in, hold it, exhale, and relax.

"Be conscious that even with the breath out, you are still alive. A lot of problems in family and social relationships are because you don't have control over the breath." —Yogi Bhajan

Yield: 1 serving

INGREDIENTS
1 cup (238 g) unsweetened vanilla coconut milk (or any dairy-free milk)
½ cup (45 g) gluten-free quick oats
1 teaspoon flaxseed meal
½ teaspoon ground cinnamon
½ teaspoon vanilla extract
¼ cup (40 g) fresh berries, plus extra to garnish
1 teaspoon sliced almonds, plus extra to garnish, or ½ tablespoon (8 g) almond butter
1 teaspoon crushed walnuts, plus extra to garnish, or ½ tablespoon (8 g) almond butter

1. In a large bowl, combine all the ingredients and mix well (alternatively, use a large mason jar, screw close, and shake it up). Chill in the refrigerator for 20 minutes while you take a shower in the morning, or for maximum creaminess, leave it overnight and have it for breakfast the following day.

2. To serve, place into individual serving bowls and garnish with extra berries and nuts—it'll make breakfast feel like a treat.

△ *"I am grounded in possibility."*

Blueberry Almond Muffins

It can be so easy for us to focus on the area of our lives that isn't flowing with as much ease as we would like; in fact, it's our ego's oldest trick because it distracts us from what is working, which is where all the magic lies. When we stop and take a minute to honor what is working, we can then bring that energy and outlook into the area we are currently struggling with. You can use this same transference principle in the kitchen. This muffin recipe happens to be one I always turn to when I'm in need of a little kitchen mojo boost because it comes out amazing every time and tastes a little like heaven.

VISUALIZATION FOR TRANSFERENCE

Sit in a comfortable position with your spine straight and your eyes closed and focused on your third-eye point (the space between your eyebrows). Take natural, long, deep breaths and call to mind an area of your life where you are really thriving. Honor whatever comes to mind first. Now, be a fly on the wall, watching how you operate in this area of your life. What basic beliefs and principles do you operate from? What kind of energy do you approach this area with? How do you feel when making decisions in this area? Take a few moments and allow yourself to play detective with your own behavior. Next, call to mind an area of your life that you are currently having trouble with. Visualize how you would operate in this area with the same principles, beliefs, and energy as you do in the area you thrive. Allow different situations to play out in your mind. Spend a few moments allowing this transference to sink in. When you are ready, take a deep breath in and hold it, allowing yourself to be fully saturated with your new confidence in this area, then exhale and relax.

Yield: 12 muffins

INGREDIENTS

Coconut oil cooking spray, for greasing (or use paper baking cups)

2 teaspoons flaxseed meal

2 tablespoons (30 ml) water

½ cup (120 ml) unsweetened almond milk

1 teaspoon apple cider vinegar

1 cup (244 g) unsweetened applesauce

½ cup (48 g) gluten-free rolled oats

½ cup (50 g) chopped almonds, plus extra for topping

⅓ cup (80 ml) maple syrup

¼ cup (37 g) date sugar

¼ cup (48 g) raw extra-virgin coconut oil, melted

2 teaspoons baking soda

1 teaspoon vanilla extract

1 teaspoon almond extract

½ teaspoon sea salt

1 cup (150 g) fresh blueberries (or frozen and slightly thawed) tossed in gluten-free flour blend

"I honor what's working."

1. Preheat the oven to 375°F (190°C, or gas mark 5) and grease a 12-cup muffin pan with cooking spray or line with paper baking cups.

2. To make flax "egg," mix together the flaxseed and water in a small bowl and set aside for 5 minutes, until thickened.

3. In a measuring cup, mix the almond milk and apple cider vinegar and set aside.

4. In a large mixing bowl, combine the flax "egg," the almond milk mixture, and the remaining ingredients (except the blueberries) and mix well. Lightly fold in the blueberries. Pour (or scoop) the batter into the muffin cups, about two-thirds full.

5. Top with the remaining almond slices. Bake for 10 to 12 minutes, or until a toothpick inserted into the center of a muffin comes out clean. Remove from the oven and set aside to cool before serving.

Cherry Rosemary Scones

I didn't realize until my mid-twenties that it was my quirks that people really loved about me. I had spent so much time trying to be "normal" and hiding the more obscure things I did or thought about from people because I wanted to impress them. It was a tremendously freeing experience when I fully embraced every aspect of my life. Are there parts of you that you're trying to smooth over for others? When playing around with different flavor combinations for these scones, I found the cherry-rosemary combo to be delightfully surprising, quirky, and well-balanced—they're not too sweet and just a little savory.

SYNCHRONIZATION MEDITATION

Sit straight. Place both hands in front of you at eye level. Extend the Jupiter (index) fingers straight up. Curl the other fingers into the palm. Keep the thumbs straight up, parallel to the index finger, thumbnails toward the body. The tip of the left index finger is held at the level of the lowest knuckle of the right thumb. Hands are 6 to 8 inches (15 to 20 cm) apart and about 1 to 11/2 feet (30 to 46 cm) in front of the face. The eyes are open, looking straight ahead and directly at and through the space between the hands. Make your breath long and slow. Continue for 11 minutes and then relax.

△ *"I embrace my quirks with love."*

Yield: 8 to 10 scones

INGREDIENTS

⅓ cup (66 g) melted raw extra-virgin coconut oil, plus 1 teaspoon for greasing
2 cups (224 g) quinoa flour
3 tablespoons (29 g) date sugar
1 tablespoon (15 ml) baking powder
Pinch of salt
1 cup (238 g) canned full-fat coconut milk
1 teaspoon vanilla extract
3 tablespoons (5 g) finely chopped fresh rosemary
1 cup (154 g) pitted cherries, halved

1. Preheat your oven to 375°F (190°C, or gas mark 5) and grease a small baking sheet (or a scone pan) with 1 teaspoon coconut oil. Set aside.

2. In a medium mixing bowl, combine all the dry ingredients and mix thoroughly, breaking up any clumps. Add the melted coconut oil, coconut milk, vanilla extract, and chopped rosemary, mix thoroughly, and then gently fold in the cherries. (The batter should be thick like a cookie dough.)

3. Roll the batter into a ball, place it on the greased baking sheet, and then press down to make a 2-inch (5 cm) thick disk. Bake for 11 to 13 minutes, or until the edges crisp and a fork comes out clean when inserted into the center. Set aside to cool for 15 minutes, and then use a sharp knife or pizza cutter to slice into 8 to 10 slices. (Alternatively, cut batter into rounds and bake.)

Brunch Tacos

A funny thing happens as you start to get the things you want: you innately start to take it for granted. I don't believe any of us really do it on purpose; we simply just up-level our problems. I call them "champagne problems"—privileged "problems" we create instead of just sitting in gratitude and appreciation for all the beautiful abundance in our lives. Regardless of where you are on your path, you are alive and reading this book right now, so you already have a ton to be grateful for. Center yourself in gratitude for your abundance and watch it multiply. Nothing makes me feel more abundant than a meal made with lots of love, and there's no meal I love more than brunch, and no food I love quite as much as tacos!

MAKE YOUR OWN GRATITUDE MEDITATION

Take out a pen and piece of paper, put on an upbeat playlist, and number your paper 1 to 100. Write down 100 things in your life you are grateful for and do not stop before reaching line 100! When you start running out of ideas, get really creative. These things can run the gamut from the big ones (being alive, your health, the well-being of your family) to the more obscure (you can afford superfood powders for your smoothies, the amazing book you're reading, the bird that stopped you in your path and made you smile). You have so much abundance in your life right now, so allow it to all flow out and be acknowledged—every last drop.

Once you're done writing your list, hit the voice recorder on your phone and speak your entire list out loud. When you are finished, save the recording as your personal gratitude practice, and when you need to get back in touch with your abundance, find a comfortable place to sit, close your eyes, take a few deep breaths, and listen to your amazing gratitude inventory.

Yield: 4 servings

INGREDIENTS

HASH BROWNS
4 sweet potatoes, peeled and cut into 1-inch (2.5 cm) square chunks
1 white onion, diced
½ red pepper, diced
½ green pepper, diced
1 tablespoon (15 ml) extra-virgin olive oil
2 teaspoons garlic powder
2 teaspoons onion powder
1 teaspoon salt

MANGO GUACAMOLE
½ red onion, diced
1 tablespoon (1 g) chopped cilantro
2 ripe avocados, halved and pitted
1 mango, diced
Juice of ½ lime
½ teaspoon salt

(continued on page 104)

 "I appreciate my abundance."

TOFU SCRAMBLED "EGGS"

1 tablespoon (15 ml) extra-virgin olive oil

14-ounce (397 g) package extra-firm tofu, drained
and crumbled

2 teaspoons ground cumin

2 teaspoons curry powder

2 teaspoons ground turmeric

2 teaspoons onion powder

2 teaspoons garlic powder

COCONUT BACON

½ cup (43 g) unsweetened coconut flakes

3 tablespoons (45 ml) tamari (gluten-free
soy sauce)

1 tablespoon (15 ml) steak seasoning

SAUTÉED KALE

3 cups (204 g) baby kale

1 clove garlic, chopped

1 tablespoon (15 ml) extra-virgin olive oil or
sesame oil

8 corn tortillas or gluten-free taco shells

1. To make the hash browns, preheat the oven to 425°F (220°C, or gas mark 7). In a medium mixing bowl, combine all the ingredients and toss well until thoroughly combined. Scatter the mixture onto a baking sheet and roast in the oven for 10 minutes, until browned and cooked through.

2. Meanwhile, to make the mango guacamole, toss the onion and cilantro in a medium bowl (or molcajete—the traditional Mexican version of the mortar and pestle) and press them into each other with the back of a spoon. In a separate bowl, lightly mash the avocado, then add it to the onion mixture along with the mango, lime juice, and salt. Mix well and set aside.

3. To make the tofu scrambled "eggs," heat the olive oil in a frying pan over medium heat. Add the tofu and spices and stir for 2 to 3 minutes until mixed through. Reduce to low heat while you complete the next steps.

4. To make the coconut bacon, combine all the ingredients in a small frying pan and spread out. Heat over medium heat and stir for 1 to 2 minutes, or until the coconut browns. Transfer the mixture to a small serving bowl.

5. Check on the hash browns, remove them from the oven, and set aside. Give the tofu scrambled eggs a good stir.

6. To make the sautéed kale, combine the baby kale, garlic, and olive oil in a medium frying pan and cook over medium heat for 3 to 5 minutes, or until the kale is bright green and wilted. Remove from the heat and place in a small bowl.

7. Place a tortilla in a dry frying pan over medium heat and cook for about 45 seconds on each side, until warm and lightly brown. Repeat with the remaining tortillas.

8. Serve all the components in separate bowls. My preferred assembly method starts with a generous helping of sautéed kale, a spoon of sweet potato hash, and topped with tofu scramble. Add a dollop of mango guacamole and a sprinkling of coconut bacon and there you have it—massive, delicious tacos that make an incredible brunch treat!

Chia Seed Pancakes

What fear has been holding you back? Your fear means well but the life of your dreams is waiting for you on the other side of that fear. Leap and the net will appear! Pancakes are perfect for helping build intuition. You have to feel when it is ready to be flipped. Sometimes it ends up perfect and other times a little messy, but as long as it's delicious, it's always salvageable—not so different from life.

KUNDALINI FOUR-STROKE BREATH TO BUILD INTUITION

Sit in a comfortable seated position and place your hands together in prayer pose. Keep your index fingers extended as you interlock all of your other fingers, clasping your hands together with your thumbs crossed. Close your eyes nine-tenths of the way and place the mudra a little below your chin where you can look at the tips of your pointing fingers through the one-tenth opening of your eyes. Inhale in four powerful strokes through your mouth shaped into an "O," or the "O" mouth, (1 stroke per second = 4-second inhale) and exhale in one powerful stroke through the nose (1 second). Continue for 16 minutes or shorten to 4 minutes if you are new to the meditation. Close the meditation with an inhale, holding the breath for 20 seconds, and stretch your arms out to the sides, palms facing upward. Exhale. Inhale deeply, hold the breath for 20 seconds, and stretch your arms horizontally and your spine vertically. Exhale. Inhale deeply, hold the breath for 20 seconds, and open up your fingers, making them like steel. Squeeze your entire energy and bring it into your arms. Exhale and relax.

Yield: 3 pancakes

INGREDIENTS

1 tablespoon (9 g) chia seeds
3 tablespoons (45 ml) water
1 cup (227 g) coconut cream yogurt
½ cup (47 g) oat bran
2 teaspoons vanilla extract
½ teaspoon ground cinnamon
2 tablespoons (24 g) raw extra-virgin coconut oil, divided
1 cup (123 g) raspberries, to serve

1. To make chia "egg," mix the ingredients together in a small bowl and set aside for 5 minutes, until thickened.

2. In a small mixing bowl, combine the chia "egg," yogurt, oat bran, vanilla extract, and cinnamon and mix well.

3. In a frying pan, heat 1 tablespoon (12 g) coconut oil over low heat. Scoop 2 tablespoons (30 g) batter into your frying pan and cook, flipping over after 3 to 4 minutes, or when batter starts bubbling. Transfer the pancake to a serving plate, and repeat with the remaining 2 pancakes.

4. Clean the frying pan, and then heat the remaining tablespoon (12 g) coconut oil over medium-high heat. Add the raspberries to the pan and heat up for 1 minute, until warmed through. The raspberries can be served on top or puréed to make a warm, sweet syrup!

"I am ready to take a leap of faith."

Crack Bars

When we create a healthy, peaceful environment inside ourselves, we can create a healthy, peaceful environment for those around us. We need to fill our cup so that it can overflow into the world, and if we are drained and depleted, everyone loses! Nourishing your mind, body, and soul has a tremendous effect on how you interact with everyone you encounter during your day. Taking care of yourself creates a ripple effect of positivity in the world. I used to be a huge fan of store-bought protein and granola bars. but once I started reading the ingredients in some of those bars, I realized that I truly wasn't taking care of myself, so I decided to make my own. These babies are called crack bars for a reason: they are super addictive, delicious, and nourishing, and perfect for a meal on the go.

BATH-TIME MEDITATION

Draw a hot bath with your favorite bath oils or salts. Light some candles and turn down the lights in your bathroom. Allow yourself to relax into the warm water, place your hands over your heart center, and close your eyes. Turn your focus to your breath and your heart space. Take long, deep breaths and allow any thoughts that come up to float on by, returning your focus inward. Ask your body, "How can I better take care of you?" and listen to what comes up. Honor whatever you may hear, and if nothing comes up right away, keep your attention at your heart center and on your breath. Relax and enjoy this loving posture. When you are ready to bring the meditation to a close, take a deep breath in and hold it, feeling the loving energy from your heart center circulate throughout your body, and then release.

Yield: 12 to 15 bars

INGREDIENTS

1 teaspoon flaxseed meal

1 tablespoon (15 ml) water

2 tablespoons (24 g) raw extra-virgin coconut oil, divided

2 cups (192 g) gluten-free oats

¾ cup (67 g) dried goji berries

⅓ cup (80 ml) brown-rice syrup

¼ cup (60 ml) unsweetened almond milk

¼ cup (40 g) hemp protein

3 tablespoons (30 g) hemp hearts

2 tablespoons (32 g) cashew butter

3 tablespoons (19 g) halved walnuts

3 tablespoons (13 g) sliced almonds

3 tablespoons (13 g) coconut flakes

3 tablespoons (26 g) chopped raw unsalted cashew nuts

3 tablespoons (12 g) pumpkin seeds

3 tablespoons (25 g) sunflower seeds

4 ounces (113 g) vegan sugar-free chocolate chips

(continued on page 108)

"I am taking care of myself."

1. To make flax "egg," mix together the flaxseed and water in a small bowl and set aside for 5 minutes, until thickened.

2. Preheat the oven to 425°F (220°C, or gas mark 7). Grease a medium baking pan with 1 tablespoon (12 g) coconut oil.

3. In a large bowl, combine the flax "egg" and remaining ingredients and mix thoroughly, until it is clumpy and granola-like in texture.

4. Pour onto the baking pan and spread evenly. Bake in the oven for 5 to 10 minutes, or until the edges begin to toast. (Keep an eye on them and be sure they do not brown.) Set aside to cool.

5. Use a sharp knife or pizza cutter to cut the granola into 12 to 15 squares.

Strawberry-Banana Gluten-Free Cakes

We have a deep desire to *feel* loved and supported. Too often we attach that feeling to outside stimuli (for example, how much our bosses praise us). Regardless of where we reach for the feeling, all roads are futile if we cannot cultivate it within ourselves. Take the time today to sit in the feeling of love and support you have inside. These oatmeal cakes are my favorite winter breakfast and feel like "a hug in your tummy." Freeze them to have on hand for a quick morning heat-up.

MEDITATION FOR A BROKEN HEART

This meditation calms the nerves and creates a state of balance within.

Sit in easy pose with a straight spine and your chin slightly tucked in. Breathe naturally. Place your palms together, lightly touching, with the tips of your Saturn (middle) fingers level with the space between your eyebrows and your forearms horizontal to the ground, elbows high. Turn your attention within. Continue for 11 minutes. To end, inhale, exhale, relax the breath, and with clasped hands stretch the arms up for 2 minutes.

Yield: 12 cakes

INGREDIENTS

Coconut oil cooking spray, for greasing
2 teaspoons flaxseed meal
2 tablespoons (30 ml) water
3 cups (270 g) gluten-free quick oats
2 ripe bananas, mashed
½ cup (83 g) chopped strawberries
½ cup (122 g) unsweetened applesauce
¼ cup (60 ml) maple syrup
1 tablespoon (15 ml) baking powder
2 teaspoons ground cinnamon
2 teaspoons vanilla extract
½ teaspoon sea salt
Warm unsweetened almond milk, to serve (optional)
Fresh berries, to garnish (optional)

1. Preheat the oven to 375°F (190°C, or gas mark 5). Grease a 12-cup muffin pan with cooking spray. Set aside.

2. To make flax "egg," mix together the flaxseed and water in a small bowl and set aside for 5 minutes, until thickened.

3. In a medium mixing bowl, combine the flax "egg," oats, bananas, strawberries, applesauce, maple syrup, baking powder, ground cinnamon, vanilla extract, and sea salt, and gently mix. Scoop the mixture into the prepared muffin pan until two-thirds full and bake for 7 to 10 minutes, or until a light crust forms on top of the oatmeal. Remove and set aside to cool.

4. Serve as is or place the baked oatmeal in a bowl of warm almond milk and garnish with fresh berries.

"I am loved and supported."

CHAPTER 8

Soups

"My patience is precious." — Cauliflower-Apple-Rosemary Soup   113

"I have the strength to persevere." — Mushroom Barley Soup   115

"I find the presents in the present." — Spaghetti Squash Noodle Soup   116

"I am the CEO of my own life." — Spinach Artichoke Soup   119

"I am ready for change." — Watermelon Gazpacho   121

"I am home." — Creamy Tomato Soup   123

"I assume the best of people." — Lentil Veggie Soup   125

"I give myself a clean slate through forgiveness." — Spicy Squash Soup   126

"I sit in the knowing that there is a way through every block." — Veggie Tom Kha Gai   127

"I am a powerful creator." — Veggie Chili   128

Cauliflower-Apple-Rosemary Soup

Patience is a virtue that I wasn't born with. A few years ago, I was listening to a Marianne Williamson lecture (Marianne Williamson is a best-selling spirtual author and lecturer), and she talked about leaving our lives up to the same force that turns the acorn into an oak tree. It finally hit me how powerful patience is. Whenever I feel my patience running low, I think about the acorn and remind myself that my patience allows the space for the magic to happen—I can trust that if I've planted the seed, nature will make the flower blossom.

KUNDALINI MEDITATION FOR THE NEGATIVE MIND

Sit in easy pose. Make a cup with your hands, your right hand cupped in your left hand, with both palms facing up. Close your eyes so that they are only slightly open, and and look down toward your cupped hands. Place this open cup at the level of your heart center and allow your elbows to relax at your sides. Inhale deeply, taking a long, steady breath through the nose. Exhale in a focused stream through rounded lips, as if you were blowing a feather out of your hands. You will feel the breath go over your hands. Let any thought or desire that is negative or persistently distracting come into your mind as you breathe. Breathe the thought and feeling in, then exhale it out with the breath. Continue for 11 minutes, gradually building to 31 minutes. Close by inhaling completely and holding the breath out as you lock in your navel point. Concentrate on each vertebra of the spine until you can feel it all the way to the base, as if it is as stiff as a rod. Inhale powerfully, exhale completely, and repeat the concentration. Repeat this final breath 3 to 5 times, then relax completely.

Yield: 4 servings

INGREDIENTS

Olive oil cooking spray, for greasing
1 head cauliflower, chopped
2 teaspoons garlic powder
2 teaspoons onion powder
Salt and freshly ground black pepper, to taste
2 apples, thinly sliced (I prefer Pink Lady apples)
2 tablespoons (30 ml) extra-virgin olive oil
1 white onion, diced
1 clove garlic, chopped
3 cups (720 g) unsweetened almond milk, divided
3 tablespoons (45 g) Dijon mustard
4 rosemary sprigs, divided

(continued on page 114)

 *"My patience is precious."*

1. Preheat the oven to 425°F (220°C, or gas mark 7). Grease a baking sheet with cooking spray. Add the cauliflower, sprinkle over the garlic and onion powders, and generously season with salt and pepper. Roast in the oven for 10 to 15 minutes, or until the cauliflower starts to brown.

2. In the meantime, grease another baking sheet with cooking spray and scatter across the apples. Bake for 5 minutes, or until the apples begin to brown.

3. Heat the olive oil in a frying pan over medium heat. Add the onion and sauté for 5 minutes until softened, then add the garlic and sauté for another minute.

4. Transfer the roasted cauliflower and apples (setting aside a few apple slices to garnish) to a food processor or high-speed blender, and then add the onions and garlic, 1 cup (240 ml) almond milk, and Dijon mustard. Pulse until puréed, gradually adding more almond milk to achieve your desired consistency.

5. Transfer the mixture into a large saucepan over medium heat, add 2 rosemary sprigs, and simmer for 10 minutes until warm and infused with rosemary. Remove the rosemary.

6. To serve, finely chop the remaining rosemary leaves. Ladle the soup into individual bowls, and then garnish with sliced apples and chopped rosemary.

Mushroom Barley Soup

It's always those days when we feel like we've hit the wall, when we don't know if we have it in us to get any further, that lead us to the biggest breakthroughs. When we silently say to ourselves, "I'm not done yet," we always prevail. Have faith that everything that is happening for you is happening for a reason; the strength you are building is beautiful, and there is nothing that is put in front of you that you don't have the resources to handle. Dig down deep into that inner well of strength and you will always persevere. And a hearty cup of soup will help build that strength!

MEDITATION FOR BURNOUT

Sit in easy pose. Raise your forearms parallel to the floor and in front of your chest. Bend your wrists down and bring them in to press the backs of your palms together, with the backs of your hands level with your chest. Your fingers are pointing down toward the floor. Fold the tips of your thumbs across your palms until they rest at the bases of your ring fingers. Let your shoulders relax and your chest lift. Gently focus your eyes at the tip of your nose. Inhale in 8 equal segments or sniffs. Exhale in 8 equal segments. Focus your attention on the sound of your breath. Continue this breathing pattern for 3 minutes, for a total of either 11 or 22 minutes. End the meditation with a deep breath in, holding it and exhaling powerfully. Relax completely.

Yield: 4 servings

INGREDIENTS

3 tablespoons (45 ml) extra-virgin olive oil

½ white onion, diced

1 clove garlic, chopped

1 cup (70 g) sliced cremini mushrooms

1 package (3.5 ounces/85 g) enoki mushrooms

1 maitake (hen of the woods) mushroom, chopped

4 cups (960 ml) mushroom broth

1 cup (157 g) cooked barley (or gluten-free quinoa)

2 cups (136 g) chopped kale

2 tablespoons (30 ml) onion powder

1½ tablespoons (23 g) fresh thyme leaves

1 tablespoon (15 ml) salt, plus extra to taste

1. Heat the olive oil in a large frying pan over medium heat. Add the onions and sauté for 5 minutes until softened, then add the garlic and sauté for another minute. Stir in the mushrooms and sauté for another 2 to 3 minutes, until the mushrooms are browned.

2. Pour in the mushroom broth, add the barley (or quinoa), kale, onion powder, thyme, and salt, and stir. Bring to to a boil, then reduce the heat, and simmer for 10 minutes. Season with more salt to taste.

△ *"I have the strength to persevere."*

Spaghetti Squash Noodle Soup

The gifts are right here. In this moment. Take a look around you. When we spend our time worrying about the future or making decisions based on the past, we are not only unhappy, but we are also not really living! Getting present in your life is the most basic, life-changing adjustment you can commit to. Right now, reading this, take a deep breath and just enjoy what is. The thing I love about making this soup is that it commands you to just be present, stirring, smelling its sweet aroma.

A LIVING MEDITATION

A living meditation is the way to live for the most blissful experience possible, but a lot of us are so out of touch with being present these days that it helps to begin in small doses. I encourage you to try a disciplined enforcement of this practice daily and transition it into a way of life. Begin by setting a timer for 30 minutes. Take a deep breath in and get really present to what is right in front of you. Maybe you are making this soup, maybe you are drinking tea and sitting on your couch; whatever it is, I want you take it in with all five senses. Pay attention to the sound of the birds outside your window, smell the squash as it comes out of the oven, enjoy the taste of each sip of tea. Be here now. And when a thought comes up that wants to distract you to what's going on later today or tomorrow, take a deep breath and bring yourself right back here, to the now.

Yield: 4 servings

INGREDIENTS

1 spaghetti squash, halved lengthwise
2 tablespoons (30 ml) extra-virgin olive oil, divided
1 onion, diced
1 clove garlic, chopped
4 cups (960 ml) vegetable broth
2 cups (136 g) baby kale
2 tablespoons (8 g) chopped fresh parsley
2 tablespoons (4 g) chopped fresh oregano
Salt and freshly ground black pepper, to taste

1. Preheat the oven to 425°F (220°C, or gas mark 7).

2. Brush the inside of the spaghetti squash with 1 tablespoon (15 ml) olive oil and lay them, facing down, on a medium baking sheet. Roast for 40 minutes, or until softened.

3. Scoop out the seeds and discard. Use a fork to scrape out the "spaghetti" strings and transfer to a bowl.

4. Heat the remaining 1 tablespoon (15 ml) olive oil in a large frying pan over medium heat. Add the onions and sauté for 5 minutes until softened, then add the garlic and sauté for another minute. Put in the spaghetti squash and cook for another 5 minutes. Pour in the vegetable broth, add the baby kale, parsley, and oregano, and stir until well mixed.

5. Bring to a boil, reduce the heat, and simmer for 10 minutes, until thoroughly warmed. Season with salt and pepper to taste.

"I find the presents in the present."

Spinach Artichoke Soup

You *are* the CEO of your own life. Your choices decide how smoothly your operation runs and how well your company does, but it also means you need to step up and own responsibility for those decisions. We all have the same amount of hours in a day: are you spending them efficiently? When you call the shots, you can make the executive decision to put in the activities that help you be the best version of you. When I was living in New York, one of my favorite late-night treats was a slice of artichoke pizza. Unfortunately, my body was not a fan of all the dairy and gluten, but my love for spinach-artichoke *anything* is satisfied with this savory, mouthwatering soup.

KUNDALINI MEDITATION FOR ABSOLUTELY POWERFUL ENERGY

"It is best to do this meditation when you have time to sleep afterwards or when you have a hard day to face . . ." —Yogi Bhajan

Sit in easy pose. Interlock all of your fingers except your ring fingers, which are pressed together pointing upward. Place the right thumb over the left thumb, locking it down. Place the mudra at diaphragm level, several inches out from your body, with your ring fingers pointing out at a 60-degree angle. Close your eyes, inhale deeply, and chant "Ong" in long form—one recitation of "Ong" per exhalation, approximately 15 seconds. (The sound is created through the nose; the mouth is held slightly open, but no air comes out through the mouth. The sound comes from the nose by way of the back of the upper palate. Your upper palate will vibrate.) Concentrate to do it correctly. Continue for 8 minutes. To close the meditation, take a deep breath in and exhale.

Yield: 4 servings

INGREDIENTS

1½ cups (170 g) frozen artichoke hearts, thawed
1½ cups (45 g) spinach leaves
2 tablespoons (30 ml) extra-virgin olive oil
1 white onion, chopped
1 garlic clove, finely chopped
1 cup (240 ml) vegetable broth, divided
2 tablespoons (14 g) quinoa flour
1½ cups (360 ml) unsweetened almond milk
⅓ cup (20 g) nutritional yeast
2 tablespoons (30 ml) lemon juice
Pinch of salt
Pinch of freshly ground black pepper
2 scallions, thinly sliced lengthwise, to garnish

(continued on page 120)

△ *"I am the CEO of my own life."*

1. Put the artichoke hearts and spinach into a food processor and pulse until finely chopped. Set aside.

2. Heat the oil in a large saucepan over medium heat. Add the onion and sauté for 5 minutes until softened, then add the garlic and sauté for another minute. Pour in ½ cup (120 ml) vegetable broth, and then rapidly stir in the flour to form a smooth paste. Add the remaining broth and the almond milk and bring to a simmer.

3. Stir in the spinach and artichoke mixture, nutritional yeast, and lemon juice. Season with salt and pepper. Simmer for another minute, stirring continuously, until heated through. Adjust the seasoning to taste.

4. To serve, ladle the soup into individual serving bowls and garnish with the scallion.

Watermelon Gazpacho

Even when we know it's in our best interest, change makes us feel vulnerable. There's a false sense of safety in staying right where we are, when in reality, the real danger is resisting change. Decide that you are ready for change and open yourself up to moving through it with love, grace, and ease. This soup inspired the topic of change because I was not into gazpachos, but I kept having the nagging feeling that I should make one myself before totally dismissing them. I put my own remix on it and ended up falling head over heels for this "out-of-my-comfort-zone" soup, and I hope you do, too!

KUNDALINI MEDITATION FOR CHANGE

Sit in easy pose with your chest lifted. With your eyes closed, start long, deep breathing, and follow the flow of your breath. Curl your fingers in as if making a fist, then bring your hands together at the center of your chest. The hands should touch lightly in two places only: the knuckles of the middle fingers and the pads of the thumbs. Your thumbs are extended toward your heart center and are pressed together. Hold this position and feel the energy across the thumbs and knuckles. It is recommended to do this meditation for 31 minutes; however, if you are just starting out, try the meditation for 5 or 11 minutes, gradually building up to a full 31-minute practice if you desire. To close, inhale deeply, exhale, and relax for 5 minutes.

"Between your two thumbs, heat will start passing. You can watch it very peacefully. It is a functional meditation." —Yogi Bhajan

Yield: 4 servings

INGREDIENTS

2 cups (304 g) chopped watermelon

2 red bell peppers, seeded and roughly chopped

1 green apple, peeled and roughly chopped, divided

1 cucumber, peeled and roughly chopped, divided

½ white onion, diced

¼ cup (60 ml) extra-virgin olive oil

2 tablespoons (30 ml) balsamic vinegar

2 tablespoons (8 g) finely chopped fresh mint, divided

1. In a blender or food processor, combine the watermelon, bell peppers, half the apple, half the cucumber, and onion. Add the olive oil, balsamic vinegar, and 1 tablespoon (4 g) chopped mint and purée until thick and smooth.

2. Pour the gazpacho into serving bowls and stir in the remaining apple and cucumber. Sprinkle over the remaining 1 tablespoon (4 g) mint. Chill before serving!

△ *"I am ready for change."*

Creamy Tomato Soup

When I first started traveling all over the world for work, I loved it; however, after about a year or so, traveling made me feel ungrounded. I would miss home, but it wasn't necessarily my apartment I was missing. One evening, I was watching the sunset and I closed my eyes to meditate and heard the message, *The only place you can ever find home is inside yourself*. And what feels more like home than some creamy tomato soup? I grew up on Campbell's and it was one of the things I missed most once I cleaned up my diet, so naturally, I had to find a way to recapture all that creamy tomato goodness.

KUNDALINI MEDITATION FOR EMOTIONAL BALANCE

This meditation is great for when you are worried, upset, or you're at a loss about what to do. Before practicing this meditation, drink a glass of water. Sit in easy pose and hug yourself, placing your palms open against your body, under your armpits. Raise your shoulders up tightly against your earlobes without cramping the neck muscles. Keep your spine straight and your chin gently tilted down in order to maintain the straight line of your spine. Close your eyes and allow your breath to slow naturally. Continue for 3 minutes, gradually building up to 11 minutes. To close the meditation, take a deep breath in, hold it, and then exhale and relax.

 *"I am home."*

Yield: 4 servings

INGREDIENTS

2 tablespoons (30 ml) extra-virgin olive oil, divided
2 white onions, diced
1 clove garlic, chopped
½ cup (65 g) raw unsalted cashew nuts, soaked in water for 2 to 3 hours and drained
½ cup (120 ml) vegetable broth
(3) 14.5-ounce (411 g) cans stewed tomatoes
½ cup (120 ml) canned light coconut milk
1 teaspoon freshly ground black pepper
¾ teaspoon salt
½ teaspoon paprika
3 tablespoons (8 g) basil leaves, shredded, to garnish

1. Heat 1 tablespoon (15 ml) olive oil in a large frying pan over medium heat. Add the onions and sauté for 5 minutes until softened, then add the garlic and sauté for another minute.

2. Transfer the mixture to a food processor or high-speed blender. Add the remaining 1 tablespoon (15 ml) olive oil, the soaked and drained cashews, vegetable broth, tomatoes, coconut milk, and spices and purée until thick and creamy.

3. Transfer the soup to a medium saucepan and heat over medium heat until the soup is warmed through. Serve hot and garnish with the basil leaves.

Lentil Veggie Soup

Yogi Bhajan famously said: "If you don't see God in all, you can't see God at all." But how often do we quickly jump to a negative conclusion about someone? Often, when we are assuming the worst of a situation, our energy shifts from being grounded or heart-centered all the way up into our heads, so we become head-centered. I have discovered that "assuming the best of people" (or a situation) is usually a good policy to operate under. The practice doesn't necessarily change the situation, but it completely shifts my energy around it and makes me feel lighter and happier once I release that heavy burden of placing a person in the wrong. This hearty soup is a great, nourishing antidote to help you ground that energy.

MEDITATION FOR SEEING INNOCENCE

Sit in a comfortable position with your palms facing up on your knees. Close your eyes and take long deep breaths. Bring the person about whom you are assuming the worst into your mind's forefront. Silently ask to see this person's innocence in the situation. Hold your gaze on them and allow the possible options for their actions to float up. Actively choose the thoughts that honor their pure goodness. If you struggle with this, call to mind their child-self. See them in the pure innocence of their three- or five-year-old self. When you are ready, take a deep breath in and send a stream of love from your heart to theirs, exhale, and come back into the room.

Yield: 4 servings

INGREDIENTS

15-ounce (425 g) can green lentils, drained
1½ carrots, chopped
1 onion, diced
1 clove garlic, finely chopped
4 cups (960 ml) vegetable broth
2 cups (136 g) chopped kale or spinach
1 cup (145 g) peas
2 tablespoons (30 ml) extra-virgin olive oil
Salt and freshly ground black pepper, to taste

1. Put the lentils in a large bowl and pour in enough boiling water to cover them. Let sit for 15 minutes, and then drain.

2. Combine all the ingredients in a large saucepan over high heat. Bring to a boil, reduce the heat, and simmer for 5 to 7 minutes, or until the carrots and onions are cooked through. Season with salt and pepper. Serve.

△ *"I assume the best of people."*

Spicy Squash Soup

How often do we let one little mistake send us off the deep end? Yes, it happened and maybe you wish it didn't, but this is NOW and you get a clean slate. When we are having trouble processing our feelings, we may also have trouble with our digestion. This soup's added little kick of spice will help you move things right along!

A MEDITATION FOR SELF-FORGIVENESS

You can do this meditation in a traditional posture like easy pose with your palms facing up or you can do it whenever you need to forgive and reset. If you are out in public or at the office, just close your eyes in a quiet place where you feel comfortable. Take a deep breath in and out. On your inhale, breathe in love, and on your exhale, release guilt or shame. Repeat for 1 to 3 minutes. Silently say to yourself: "I forgive myself for what I have done and choose to do better. I choose to begin again with a clean slate." Take a deep breath in and hold it, filling yourself up with love and forgiveness, exhale, and relax. Repeat as often as necessary if feelings of guilt, shame, or "ruining it" come up.

Yield: 4 servings

INGREDIENTS

2 tablespoons (24 g) raw extra-virgin coconut oil
1 acorn squash, halved lengthwise and seeded
2 red peppers, seeded and coarsely chopped
2 tablespoons (30 ml) extra-virgin olive oil
1 onion, diced
1 clove garlic, chopped
2 cups (480 ml) vegetable broth
½ teaspoon chili powder
½ teaspoon ground cumin
½ teaspoon ground coriander
½ teaspoon curry powder
½ teaspoon paprika
½ teaspoon ground turmeric
Salt and freshly ground black pepper, to taste

1. Preheat the oven to 425°F (220°C, or gas mark 7). Grease 2 medium baking sheets with coconut oil.

2. Slice 1 inch (2.5 cm) from the bottom of each acorn squash so that they sit flat on a prepared baking sheet. Scatter the peppers on the other baking sheet. Roast both for 20 minutes, until the squash has softened and the peppers get color. Set aside.

3. Meanwhile, heat the olive oil in a large frying pan over medium heat. Add the onions and sauté for 5 minutes until softened, then add the garlic and sauté for another minute. Transfer the mixture to a high-speed blender or food processor, and then add the vegetable broth and spices.

4. Once the squash are cool enough to handle, trim off the skin from the squash and cut both into chunks. Add the squash and peppers to the blender or food processor and purée until smooth and creamy.

5. Season with salt and pepper, transfer the soup to a saucepan, and heat over medium heat until warmed through. Serve.

 "I give myself a clean slate through forgiveness."

Veggie Tom Kha Gai

Even though, at times, we may not know how to get around a block, we have the choice to sit in the knowledge that there is always a way through. You can handle this. Give yourself some silence and go inward, ask for a sign or guidance on how to best navigate your current situation, and then honor what your inner GPS is telling you. This soup recipe came about after I found my way through one of my own blocks. Thai cooking really used to intimidate me. This book was just the nudge I needed to get playing in the kitchen, and once I got out of my own way, magic was made.

KUNDALINI INNER CONFLICT RESOLVER REFLEX MEDITATION

Sit in easy pose, with your eyes closed nine-tenths of the way. Place your hands over your chest, with your palms on your torso at the level of the breasts and your fingers pointing toward each other across the chest. The key to this meditation is attention to the breath. Inhale deeply and completely for 5 seconds. Exhale completely for 5 seconds. Hold the breath out for 15 seconds, by suspending the chest motion as you pull in your navel point and abdomen. Begin with 11 minutes, gradually building up to 31 or 62 minutes if you feel called. To close, take a deep inhale and stretch your arms up over your head. Relax the breath and shake your arms and hands for 15 to 30 seconds. Relax.

△ "I sit in the knowing that there is a way through every block."

Yield: 4 servings

INGREDIENTS

3 cups (720 ml) vegetable broth
2 stalks lemongrass, cut into 1-inch sections
1 white onion, thinly sliced
4-inch (10 cm) piece galangal or ginger root, thinly sliced
2 cups (476 ml) canned coconut milk
3 bird's-eye chiles, halved
Juice of 1 lime
1 cup (70 g) chopped cremini mushrooms
3 tablespoons (45 ml) tamari (gluten-free soy sauce)
3 tablespoons (3 g) chopped cilantro, plus extra for garnish
Tofu chunks or rice noodles (optional)

1. In a large saucepan, combine the vegetable broth, lemongrass, onion, and galangal and bring to a boil over medium heat. Reduce the heat and simmer for 2 to 3 minutes, stirring continuously. Add the coconut milk, chiles, lime juice, mushrooms, tamari, and cilantro and continue to simmer for another 5 to 7 minutes. Add tofu or rice noodles, if using.

2. Ladle into individual bowls, garnish with cilantro, and serve hot. If you don't want the soup to be fiery hot, remove the chiles before serving.

Veggie Chili

You are so powerful that you have created the reality you are living in through your thoughts, feelings, and subconscious patterns—even that somewhat funky area in your life. So maybe that's the bad news, but it's also the good news because you have the power to flip the switch and create whatever it is you want for your life using the tools in this book. The beauty of making chili is that it's pretty hard to mess it up. You can choose what to put in and leave out—kind of like life, if you think about it.

MY IDEAL DAY VISUALIZATION

I suggest following up this exercise with a journaling session. Jot down any details you noticed that you can start incorporating into your life right now.

In this exercise, I invite you to blow the roof off what you think is possible for your life. Really allow your mind to go where it wants and honor your deep, even childhood, desires, hopes, dreams, etc. Have fun with it and you will gain some incredible insights. Find a comfortable spot to sit with your eyes closed and your palms facing up. Bring your focus inward, taking long, deep breaths, and imagine yourself waking up in the morning to your "ideal day." Visualize your bedroom, what does it look like? Take in the excitement you feel starting your day. Now, make your way through your day, acting like a fly on the wall and observing as many details as possible: your morning routine, your outfit, your job, your dinner, and your nighttime routine. Take a moment to inhale deeply and hold it, allowing yourself to be filled with all the gratitude you have for your day. Exhale. Slowly wiggle your hands and toes and come back into the room.

Yield: 4 servings

INGREDIENTS

2 tablespoons (30 ml) extra-virgin olive oil
1 red onion, diced
4 garlic cloves, chopped
2 tablespoons (30 ml) chili powder
2 teaspoons ground cumin
1½ teaspoons smoked paprika
1 teaspoon dried oregano
2 carrots, chopped
1 large green pepper, seeded and chopped
28-ounce (800 g) can diced tomatoes
1 bay leaf
15-ounce (425 g) can black beans, rinsed and drained
15-ounce (425 g) can kidney beans rinsed and drained
2 cups (480 ml) vegetable broth
1 cup (140 g) chopped butternut squash
1 cup (68 g) chopped kale
1 to 2 teaspoons lime juice, to taste
Salt and freshly ground black pepper, to taste
2 tablespoons (2 g) chopped cilantro, to garnish

1. Heat the oil in a large saucepan over medium heat. Add the onions and sauté for 5 minutes until softened, then add the garlic and sauté for another minute. Stir in the chili powder, cumin, paprika, and oregano and cook for 1 to 2 minutes.

2. Add the remaining ingredients and bring to a boil over high heat. Reduce the heat and simmer for 15 to 20 minutes, stirring occasionally, until the carrots and squash are tender. Season with salt and pepper, transfer to a serving bowl, and garnish with cilantro.

 *"I am a powerful creator."*

CHAPTER 9

Salads and Bowls

"I release my excuses and step into my power." — Shaved Brussels Sprout Salad   133

"My inner peace creates peace in the world around me." — Taco Salad with Chili-Lime Ranch Dressing   135

"I honor my inner voice." — California Kale Salad   137

"I am bountiful, blissful, and beautiful." — Yogi Bowl   138

"My health is my greatest wealth." — Tofu Kale Waldorf Salad   140

"I am grounded and steady." — Grounding Salad   142

"When I get overwhelmed, I go back to basics." — Tomato Arugula Salad   145

"I am connected to everything." — The Rooted Bowl   147

"I create momentum through action." — Asian Broccoli Slaw   149

"It's possible to have the best of both worlds." — Caesar Salad   150

Shaved Brussels Sprout Salad

Your excuses are weighing you down and draining your energy, but, at any moment, you can step into your power simply by making a decision. Whether you decide to fully commit to something or not, either way, there is a clear and honest decision. When you are in your power, you make choices; when you are in victim mode, you make excuses. Growing up, I had a strong resistance to Brussels sprouts. My mom used to boil them and call them "martian heads," which made me detest them even more. When I was teaching myself how to cook vegetables, I made a decision to make these "martian heads" delicious, and now I'm a full-blown addict.

MEDITATION FOR RELEASING

Find a comfortable place to sit with your palms facing up and your eyes closed. Take a deep breath in through your nose and exhale out your mouth. Allow yourself to indulge in the breath and feel it moving through your body, with each breath releasing any tension or stress you are holding. Feel where in your body you are tight or knotted up and breathe into that spot and allow it to release with each exhale. Now bring to mind a situation you have been making a lot of excuses about and ask to see it clearly. Take a few more deep breaths and honor anything that might come up for you around this situation. Allow any and all excuses you have been making to come to the forefront of your mind, and with each exhale, breathe out each excuse and expel it from your being—inhaling the excuse, exhaling and tossing it out of your mind and into the air. Repeat as many times as necessary until you find yourself running out of your excuses and come back once again to the original circumstance at stake and ask to see it clearly. Sit and take some long, deep breaths and honor what you see or hear in this moment. When you are ready, take a deep breath in and hold it, then exhale and relax.

Yield: 2 servings

INGREDIENTS

2 tablespoons (30 ml) extra-virgin olive oil
½ onion, diced
1 clove garlic, finely chopped
2 cups (176 g) Brussels sprouts, quartered
1 teaspoon ground turmeric
1 teaspoon garlic powder
1 teaspoon onion powder
Salt and freshly ground black pepper, to taste
½ head romaine lettuce, chopped
1 cup (260 g) cannellini beans, rinsed and drained
1 cup (151 g) sliced grapes
2 tablespoons (13 g) chopped walnuts, to garnish

1. Heat the oil in a large saucepan over medium heat. Add the onions and sauté for 5 minutes until softened, then add the garlic and sauté for another minute. Add the Brussels sprouts, turmeric, garlic powder, and onion powder, and mix well. Season with salt and pepper to taste, then reduce the heat to low and set aside to continue cooking.

2. Combine the lettuce, cannellini beans, and grapes in a large bowl. Add the Brussels sprout mixture and toss well. Place in individual serving bowls and garnish with the walnuts.

 "I release my excuses and step into my power."

Taco Salad with Chili-Lime Ranch Dressing

Our inner peace is powerful when it comes not only to navigating the circumstances and situations in our lives but also to shifting the energy going on around us in the world. The more of us that are at peace in our individual lives, the more peaceful people in the world and the less hatred and violence will exist. Your power when handling any situation comes from your inner peace, so I'm excited to provide you with this short and simple meditation to bring you back home in moments of frustration. One of the areas where I needed peace was in the kitchen, so I started small, making easy and accessible meals, and then slowly built up my kitchen mojo and got a little more creative.

PEACE BEGINS WITH ME KUNDALINI MEDITATION

You can do this meditation sitting in easy pose or while you are standing in the checkout line at the grocery store—whenever and wherever you need to remind yourself that peace begins with you!

Close your eyes, if possible, then gently press your thumb against your index finger, followed by your middle finger, ring finger, and pinkie, repeating the mantra "Peace. Begins. With. Me."

Touch your index finger and say, "Peace."
Touch your middle finger and say, "Begins."
Touch your ring finger and say, "With."
Touch your pinkie and say, "Me."

Breathe deeply as you say each word, and go at your own pace. Repeat this as long as needed to bring you back to a centered, peaceful mind. I find that it works wonders in just a minute or two.

△ *"My inner peace creates peace in the world around me."*

Yield: 2 servings

INGREDIENTS

¼ cup (41 g) precooked chickpeas, drained and rinsed

½ cup (51 g) walnuts

2 tablespoons (30 ml) extra-virgin olive oil

1 teaspoon flaxseed meal

½ teaspoon ground cumin

½ teaspoon ground coriander

½ teaspoon paprika

½ teaspoon chili powder

½ teaspoon garlic powder

½ teaspoon onion powder

Salt and freshly ground black pepper, to taste

½ tomato, chopped

½ white onion, diced

¼ cup (4 g) chopped cilantro

1 jalapeño, chopped and divided

4 romaine lettuce leaves, chopped

½ cup (97 g) precooked black beans, drained and rinsed

1 avocado, halved, pitted, and sliced

(continued on page 136)

CHILI-LIME RANCH DRESSING

¼ cup (60 g) tofu sour cream (This can be
substituted with homemade cashew sour
cream: prepare the Creamy Cashew Yogurt
recipe on page 93 and add more lemon juice,
to taste.)
Juice from ¼ lime
Pinch of onion powder
Pinch of parsley
Pinch of garlic powder
Pinch of chili powder
½ teaspoon plain unsweetened almond milk

1. In a food processor, combine the chickpeas,
   walnuts, olive oil, flaxseed meal, cumin,
   coriander, paprika, chili powder, garlic powder,
   and onion powder. Generously season with salt
   and pepper and pulse until the mixture has the
   consistency of chopped "meat." Set aside.

2. In a small bowl, combine the tomatoes, onion,
   cilantro, and a teaspoon of jalapeño and toss
   together.

3. Place the chopped romaine lettuce into
   2 individual serving bowls. To each bowl,
   add a spoonful black beans, 2 spoonfuls of
   tomato mixture, a spoonful of the chopped
   "meat," and sliced avocado.

4. To make the chili-lime ranch dressing,
   combine all the ingredients in a bowl, mix
   together, and drizzle over salad.

California Kale Salad

Honoring my inner voice has been and always will be my number one secret to creating a life that lights me up, and my inner voice encouraged me to move to California. The weather is almost always warm and I love tossing together a light and nourishing salad to get me through the afternoon. This recipe is your quintessential kale salad with my personal spin on it, a combination of all my favorite things: creamy avocado, crunchy nuts, sweet berries, and light and tangy homemade vinaigrette.

INTUITIVE MEDITATION AND WRITING EXERCISE

Grab a pen and paper, or your journal, and find a comfortable spot. Write down a question relating to something going on in your life that you've been feeling lost at sea about. Now close your eyes, place your palms face up, and bring your attention to your natural breathing. Imagine a ray of light coming down from the sky, into the top of your head, or your crown chakra, and pouring its beam of light into your heart center. With each breath, see this light filling you up, charging you with its energy. Continue for 3 minutes. At the end of the 3 minutes, take a deep breath in and hold it, feeling the light saturate every particle of your being, then exhale. Now immediately put your pen to paper and answer your question. Don't think; just allow your hand to move with the pen on paper and let whatever is coming forth flow outward. Keep writing until you feel complete and then go back and look at the guidance you have received on the matter by allowing your inner voice to hold the pen.

"I honor my inner voice."

Yield: 2 servings

INGREDIENTS

DRESSING
2 heaping tablespoons (30 g) tahini
2 heaping tablespoons (30 g) Dijon mustard
¼ cup (60 ml) extra-virgin olive oil
¼ cup (60 ml) balsamic vinegar

½ white onion, chopped
1 tablespoon (15 ml) extra-virgin olive oil
2 cups (136 g) chopped kale
3 tablespoons (19 g) chopped walnuts, plus extra for garnish
3 tablespoons (13 g) sliced almonds, plus extra for garnish
2 tablespoons (20 g) hemp hearts
1 avocado, halved, pitted, and sliced
½ cup (83 g) chopped strawberries

1. To make the dressing, combine all ingredients in a small bowl and whisk together until creamy. Set aside.

2. Add the onion to a small saucepan with the olive oil over medium heat. Sauté the onion by moving it around with a spatula until it is soft and starts to brown.

3. In a large bowl, combine the remaining ingredients, drizzle over the dressing, and toss until the salad is thoroughly dressed. Transfer to a serving bowl and garnish with the nuts.

Yogi Bowl

Our self-esteem comes from within. It's not something that we cultivate through outside achievements or attractiveness. We need to cultivate a healthy amount of self-esteem to truly show up in the world as our highest selves in everything we do, so it's incredibly important to have a daily practice that fills you up so you can shine bright all day long. I'm a huge lover of the "yogi bowl." When it comes to getting in the kitchen, we may feel pressure to make a "real meal" and whip out something fancy. Well, the yogi bowl gives you permission to put together a few of your favorite things in a bowl and call it a meal. It's great for leftovers and for making healthy choices when you are short on time.

KUNDALINI MANTRA FOR SELF-ESTEEM

When I first started practicing meditation and an exercise would come up that would require us to sing this mantra, I found it to be silly. But once I gave over to it (and got over myself), I realized that I can't help but feel tremendously happy after repeating it many times.

You can choose to do this exercise as a standard meditation and a living meditation. For the standard version, sit comfortably, close your eyes, and focus on your third-eye point (the space between your eyebrows), and repeat: "I am bountiful, blissful, and beautiful. Bountiful, blissful, and beautiful, I am." There are also great recordings you can sing along with if that is your thing. Continue for anywhere from 3 to 11 minutes and then take a deep breath in, hold it, and exhale. As a living meditation, bring this mantra with you wherever you go, silently in your head, repeating: "I am bountiful, blissful, and beautiful. Bountiful, blissful, and beautiful, I am." It's a great counter-attack to negative self-talk. When you hear it come up, bring up the mantra and replace whatever non-loving thoughts with this simple mantra.

Yield: 2 servings

INGREDIENTS

DIJON VINAIGRETTE
¼ cup (60 ml) extra-virgin olive oil
¼ cup (60 g) Dijon mustard
2 tablespoons (30 ml) balsamic vinegar
2 tablespoons (20 g) freshly grated horseradish
Salt and freshly ground black pepper, to taste
Grade B maple syrup (optional, for a maple-Dijon dressing), to taste

1 cup (185 g) cooked quinoa
1 avocado, halved, pitted, and diced
2 cups (272 g) steamed veggies such as broccoli, cauliflower, or zucchini (you can use fresh, frozen, or a steam-bag option)
1 cup (185 g) precooked black beans, rinsed, drained and warmed

1. To make my favorite Dijon vinaigrette, combine all the ingredients in a small bowl and whisk until creamy.

2. Combine all the other ingredients in a bowl, drizzle over the dressing, and toss. Serve. (Alternatively, serve the dressing on the side.)

△ *"I am bountiful, blissful, and beautiful."*

Tofu Kale Waldorf Salad

Waking up every day with a heart that's beating steadily, lungs that can breathe in fresh air, and a body that can stand up and get out of bed is truly an immense blessing. The more you attune yourself to being healthy, the more you will appreciate it, take care of it, and put what is truly important first. Loving and accepting our body also releases a lot of temptation to put things in our body that we know may harm it. It's important to find out what works for you and honor it. I found what didn't work for me in a harsh way, so I set out to make "body-friendly" versions of dishes I loved, such as this salad.

BODY LOVE MEDITATION

Find a comfortable place and sit or lie down. Close your eyes and bring your attention to your breath. Take long, deep breaths and allow yourself to be extremely present in your body. Sit in the gratitude you have for simply being alive today, for having the opportunity to walk this earth, to enjoy the company of others, and to do the beautiful work you came here to do. Take a moment and center on your heart. Feel it beating and allow yourself to sit in immense gratitude for the blood it pumps through your body, for its constant beating without any help from you. Now focus back on your breath and fill yourself up with gratitude for the following body functions as you did with your heart: your respiratory system; your nervous system; your skin, muscles, and skeleton; your blood; your digestive system; your reproductive system; and your endocrine system. Finally, take a moment and just allow yourself to saturate in the deep love and gratitude you have for your body in this minute. Take a deep breath in, hold it as you feel that love seeping into every cell of your being, and exhale.

Yield: 4 servings

INGREDIENTS

DRESSING
(2) 8-ounce (226 g) containers dairy-free coconut yogurt
½ cup (30 g) fresh parsley, finely chopped
1 teaspoon ground oregano
Salt and freshly ground black pepper, to taste
Juice of 2 lemons

2 tablespoons (30 ml) extra-virgin olive oil
16-ounce (453 g) package firm tofu, drained and cut into 3-inch (7.5 cm) cubes
⅓ cup (80 g) Dijon mustard
2 tablespoons (30 ml) garlic powder
Salt and freshly ground black pepper, to taste
4 cups (272 g) chopped kale
1 Granny Smith apple, very thinly sliced
1 cup (151 g) sliced grapes
½ cup (51 g) chopped walnuts

△ *"My health is my greatest wealth."*

1. To make the dressing, combine the yogurt, parsley, oregano, and salt and pepper, and mix well. Stir in the lemon juice. Set aside.

2. Heat the oil in a medium frying pan over medium heat. Add the tofu, mustard, garlic powder, salt, and pepper and cook for 5 to 7 minutes, stirring occasionally. Reduce the heat to low and continue to cook while you prepare the rest of the salad (keeping an eye on the pan throughout).

3. Put the kale and dressing in a large bowl and massage the dressing into the leaves for a few minutes. (This softens the kale and distributes the dressing evenly!) Add the sliced apples, grapes, and walnuts.

4. Add the tofu to the salad mixture and toss. Serve.

Grounding Salad

When we are ungrounded, it feels like chaos; all the thoughts in our heads are swirling, we don't feel solid or at peace, and we don't make the best decisions because we're not thinking clearly. By connecting back to nature and eating more root vegetables and warm foods, we bring ourselves back to a steady, more powerful place. Roasting vegetables—especially root vegetables—gives them a grounding energy, which has an incredible power to connect us back to the earth's core. This salad is a great balance of both: it not only quenches the desire for the greens of a salad, but it also includes hearty roasted veggies, such as Brussels sprouts, carrots, and potatoes, along with lots of great spices, to bring you back down into your root chakra.

DOWN TO EARTH MEDITATION

Ideally, you would do this meditation on a nice patch of grass or perhaps sitting on the beach; however, you can still connect yourself to the center of the earth in just a few minutes right in the comfort of your home. Find a comfortable place to sit in easy pose, close your eyes, and start focusing on your breath—in through your nose and out your mouth. Bring your attention to where you are sitting on the floor and imagine a thick rope extending out of your being, all the way down and around the core of the earth, anchoring you to it. Feel that rope crystallize and strengthen, all the way from the base of your spine into the earth's core. Take a moment to really embrace this connected, anchored, and supported feeling, knowing that you are being held so powerfully by this planet, and then carry that with you through-out your day. Sit anywhere from 3 to 20 minutes. When you are ready to release and end the med-itation, gently move your fingers and toes, rub your palms together, and place them over your eye sockets as your slowly open your eyes and expose them to the light.

Yield: 2 servings

INGREDIENTS

5 tablespoons (75 ml) extra-virgin olive oil, divided

4 baby potatoes, sliced (I prefer the colored ones but any kind will do!)

1 teaspoon dried oregano

2 teaspoons fine sea salt, divided

2 teaspoons garlic powder, divided

2 teaspoons onion powder, divided

½ cup (44 g) quartered Brussels sprouts

1 clove garlic, thinly sliced

1 shallot, thinly sliced

¼ cup (31 g) sliced carrot

2 teaspoons slivered almonds

1 teaspoon ground turmeric

1 teaspoon curry powder

1 teaspoon ground coriander

1 cup (68 g) chopped kale

1 cup (29 g) spring mix salad

(continued on page 144)

"I am grounded and steady."

1. Preheat the oven to 425°F (220°C, or gas mark 7). Lightly grease 2 baking sheets with 2 tablespoons (30 ml) olive oil and set aside.

2. In a small bowl, combine the potatoes, oregano, 1 tablespoon (15 ml) olive oil, and 1 teaspoon each of the salt, garlic, and onion powder and mix until thoroughly coated. Transfer the potatoes to one of the prepared baking sheets and roast for 10 minutes, or until the edges turn crisp and golden brown.

3. Meanwhile, combine the Brussels sprouts and 1 tablespoon (15 ml) olive oil in a small bowl and toss with the remaining 1 teaspoon salt, garlic powder, and onion powder. Arrange them on the other prepared baking sheet and roast in the oven for 5 to 7 minutes, or until the edges turn crisp and golden brown.

4. Heat the remaining 1 tablespoon (15 ml) olive oil in a frying pan over medium heat. Add the garlic and shallot and sauté for 1 minute until fragrant. Add the sliced carrots, almonds, turmeric, curry powder, and ground coriander, reduce the heat, and lightly sauté for several minutes, until the shallots and garlic are browned.

5. Divide the kale and spring mix between 2 individual serving bowls. Add the roasted potatoes and Brussels sprouts, and then finish with the carrot mixture.

Tomato Arugula Salad

Feeling overwhelmed had been a pattern that had run rampant in my life for years. One day, when I was scrolling through Facebook, I saw a post about priorities, so I scribbled my top three personal priorities and my top three work priorities on a Post-It. Then I stuck those lists on my fridge. For the next couple of weeks, whenever I felt overwhelmed, I'd reference the Post-It. I went back to basics—what's really important to me—and I allowed the excess to be released with a polite "no thank you." Since then, I've allowed my "basics" to be my guiding light. I love this salad because of its simplicity, and when you are eating fresh, nutrient-dense food, you don't have to do much to it. You can just let it shine.

BASIC BREATH

The basics start with your breath. Use this whenever or wherever you are as a simple tool to bring you back home.

Close your eyes and relax your face and your shoulders. Take a deep breath in through your nose and out your mouth and just focus your attention on the breath. Allow any thoughts that come up to pass by, returning your attention to your breath. Feel the breath circulate throughout your entire being as it goes in your nose and out your mouth. Continue for 3 minutes or as long as you want.

Yield: 4 servings

INGREDIENTS

Coconut oil cooking spray, for greasing
1 cup (160 g) wild rice
2 cups (474 ml) water
1 cup (149 g) grape tomatoes, halved
Salt and freshly ground black pepper, to taste
5 tablespoons (75 ml) extra-virgin olive oil, divided
½ white onion, thinly sliced
3 cloves garlic, chopped
4 cups (80 g) arugula
3 tablespoons (45 ml) balsamic vinegar
2 tablespoons (4 g) chopped fresh oregano
2 tablespoons (6 g) chopped fresh basil

1. Preheat the oven to 425°F (220°C, or gas mark 7). Lightly grease a medium baking sheet with cooking spray. Set aside.

2. Put the wild rice and water in a medium saucepan and bring to a boil. Reduce the heat and simmer for 40 minutes, covered, or until cooked through.

3. Meanwhile, put the tomatoes on the prepared baking sheet and season with salt and pepper. Roast for 10 minutes, or until softened.

4. Heat 1 tablespoon (15 ml) olive oil in a small frying pan over medium heat. Add the onions and sauté for 5 minutes until softened, then add the garlic and sauté for another minute. Set aside.

5. Drain the wild rice. In a large bowl, combine the arugula, wild rice, roasted tomatoes, garlic and onion mixture, oregano and basil and mix well. Season with remaining olive oil and salt and pepper to taste, transfer to a platter, and serve.

"When I get overwhelmed, I go back to basics."

The Rooted Bowl

There is no greater power than realizing we are all one. We are made from the same tiny particles. We are interconnected. Your energy and actions create a ripple effect because just as you are one person in the world, you are the world in one person. Sometimes when I'm doing a lot of meditation and yoga or eating a lot of raw foods, I can start to feel ungrounded, almost like I'm floating in the clouds, physically and mentally. Eating this bowl filled with lots of roasted root veggies literally brings me down to earth and helps me feel strong and focused.

INTERCONNECTEDNESS MEDITATION

Get outside if possible: go to a park, the beach, or someplace where you feel peaceful and connected to the earth. If that's not possible, you can do it in the comfort of your home. Sit comfortably with your spine straight and your eyes closed. Rest your palms face up on your knees. Take a deep breath in through your nose and out your mouth. Take a few long, deep breaths, allowing any tension or stress from the day to release from your body. Bring your focus to your sitting bones; feel them supporting you and imagine a root growing out of your spine and reaching all the way to the core of the earth, wrapping itself around the center of the earth and anchoring you in. Feel it supporting you and holding you. Now bring your focus to the top of your head. Feel a warm, white light pouring down from above and coming in through the crown of your head, filling your body with its warmth and light. Allow yourself to sit in this space, being held from both directions, filled with light and anchored to the earth all at once. Sit for a few more moments soaking it all in. When you are ready, take a deep breath in and hold it, filling yourself with this feeling of rooted light. Exhale and relax.

Yield: 2 servings

INGREDIENTS

Coconut oil cooking spray, for greasing
1 cup (100 g) cauliflower florets
1 cup (100 g) broccoli florets
Salt and freshly ground black pepper, to taste
2 tablespoons (30 ml) extra-virgin olive oil, divided
1 bunch asparagus spears, trimmed
2 cloves garlic, finely chopped
3 tablespoons (13 g) sliced almonds
1 small white onion, diced
2 teaspoons ground turmeric
2 teaspoons ground coriander
2 teaspoons curry powder
½ teaspoon paprika
15-ounce (425 g) can chickpeas, rinsed
    and drained

(continued on page 148)

△ *"I am connected to everything."*

1. Preheat the oven to 425°F (220°C, or gas mark 7). Lightly grease 1 large or 2 medium baking sheets with the cooking spray.

2. Spread out your cauliflower and broccoli on the baking sheet(s). Lightly season with salt and pepper each and roast for 15 minutes.

3. Meanwhile, heat 1 tablespoon (15 ml) olive oil in a frying pan over medium heat. Add the asparagus and cook for 3 to 4 minutes, until they turn bright green. Add the garlic and almonds and sauté for another minute. Transfer the asparagus to a bowl.

4. Using the same frying pan, heat the remaining 1 tablespoon (15 ml) olive oil over medium heat. Add the onion, turmeric, coriander, curry, and paprika and cook for 2 to 3 minutes. Stir in the chickpeas, mix well so that they are covered in the spices, and cook for another 5 minutes. Set aside.

5. Remove the roasted broccoli and cauliflower from the oven and put them into individual serving bowls. (Alternatively, put the cauliflower in a food processor and pulse a few times until it has a rice-like consistency, as shown in the photograph. Then place the rice and broccoli in your bowls.)

6. To serve, scatter over the chickpeas and top with the asparagus.

Asian Broccoli Slaw

The first step is always the hardest, but once you take it, little by little the resistance loosens its grip until you eventually gain momentum in the direction you want to go. Where in your life do you feel stuck right now? Take the first step and allow your action to create momentum around the things that light you up. This delicious dish can help you create momentum in the kitchen. Not only is it nourishing and satisfying, but it's also creative enough to get your culinary juices flowing.

KUNDALINI MEDITATION FOR ADDICTIONS

This meditation is great for busting through blocks, creating momentum, and freeing us from the subconscious thought patterns and habits that we are addicted to but that aren't serving us. It's the first meditation I do each morning to ease into my practice.

Sit in easy pose with your eyes closed and focus on your third-eye point (the space between your eyebrows). Make fists with both of your hands and extend the thumbs out straight. Place your thumbs on your temples and find the niches where your thumbs fit in. Lock your upper and lower molars together and keep your lips closed. Keeping your teeth pressed together through-out, alternately squeeze the molars tightly and then release the pressure. Muscles will move in rhythm under your thumbs. Feel them massage the thumbs and apply pressure to the temples with your hands. Silently vibrate the four primal sounds, "sa ta na ma." Continue for 3 minutes, then take a deep breath in and hold it. Exhale and bring your hands down.

"I create momentum through action."

Yield: 2 servings

INGREDIENTS

DRESSING

¼ cup (60 ml) macadamia nut oil (or extra-virgin olive oil)
3 tablespoons (45 ml) rice vinegar
3 tablespoons (45 ml) sesame oil
3 tablespoons (45 ml) shoyu (or soy sauce)
3 cloves garlic, finely chopped
1 tablespoon (6 g) chopped scallion
1 tablespoon (6 g) grated fresh ginger

12-ounce (340 g) bag broccoli slaw
¼ cup (50 g) shelled edamame
¼ cup (10 g) shredded radicchio
¼ cup (18 g) slivered almonds, plus extra to garnish
¼ cup (27 g) shredded carrot, plus extra to garnish
½ cup (93 g) cooked quinoa

1. Put the broccoli slaw, edamame, radicchio, almonds, and carrots in a large bowl and toss to mix.

2. To make the dressing, combine all the ingredients and whisk. Drizzle enough dressing into the bowl of slaw so that the slaw is damp but not soaked. Put the quinoa on a plate and top with the broccoli slaw mixture. Garnish with almond slivers and carrots, if desired.

Caesar Salad

You may be faced with a situation where you feel like you need to choose between two things that are important to you. Allow yourself, for a minute, to hold the possibility of having the best of both worlds. I call this "making space for the miracle." When I first went vegan, one of the things I was most upset about was having to pass on my favorite salad. Well, once I took myself above the battlefield and got a fresh perspective, I realized I could create the same textures and flavor using ingredients that I love!

ABOVE THE BATTLEFIELD MEDITATION

Close your eyes and focus on your breath. Allow a situation to come to mind where you feel like you are being pulled in two directions. You think you need to sacrifice X to have Y, and as you bring it to mind, allow yourself to float above it and see the situation from your higher self. Is there a way to navigate the situation with love and creativity? If something doesn't come to mind right away, don't be discouraged—sometimes, we get attached to our way of thinking about a situation and need to take a few moments to surrender and ask for the miracle, demand a shift in perspective, and a look from above the battlefield!

Yield: 2 servings

INGREDIENTS

½ cup (76 g) canned chickpeas, rinsed and drained
1 teaspoon extra-virgin olive oil, plus extra
2 teaspoons curry powder
1 teaspoon ground coriander
1 teaspoon ground turmeric
1 teaspoon garlic powder
Salt and freshly ground black pepper, to taste
¼ cup sliced (18 g) or whole (35 g) almonds
1 tablespoon (15 g) nutritional yeast
1 head romaine lettuce, leaves separated and
   coarsely chopped
1 avocado, halved, pitted, and sliced

DRESSING

1 tablespoon (15 g) garlic hummus
1 tablespoon (15 ml) extra-virgin olive oil
4 cloves garlic, crushed
Juice of ½ lemon
1 teaspoon dried oregano

1. Preheat the oven to 425°F (220°C, or gas mark 7). Line 2 baking sheets with parchment paper and set aside.

2. In a medium mixing bowl, combine the chickpeas, olive oil, curry powder, coriander, turmeric, garlic powder, salt, and pepper and toss until the chickpeas are thoroughly coated. Transfer the mixture to one of the prepared baking sheets and roast for 10 minutes, stirring occasionally, until they start to brown.

3. Meanwhile, combine the almonds and nutritional yeast in a small bowl and toss until the almonds are thoroughly coated. (Add a teensy bit of olive oil to help it stick, if necessary.) Spread on the second prepared baking sheet. Roast in the oven for 7 to 9 minutes, or until lightly browned.

4. To make the dressing, combine all the ingredients in a small bowl and whisk until creamy. Season with salt and pepper.

5. Put the chopped lettuce in a salad bowl, add the dressing, and toss lightly. Top with the roasted almonds and chickpeas and sliced avocado. Serve.

△ "It's possible to have the best of both worlds."

CHAPTER 10

Entrées

"I release everything that is not serving me." — Veggie Curry   154

"I welcome a new beginning." — Mushroom Tacos   156

"I am willing to see things differently." — Cauliflower Fried Rice   159

"I handle all situations with grace and courage." — Grandma's Galumpkis (Stuffed Cabbage Rolls)   161

"I receive clarity through simplicity." — Spaghetti Squash with Fresh Herbs   163

"I am nourished by my passion." — Mexican Quinoa Avocado Boats   165

"I release the need to be perfect." — Best Veggie Burger Ever and Avocado Fries   167

"I feel loved and supported." — Lentil Shepherd's Pie   170

"I am in love with the little things." — Brussels Sprout Tacos   172

"I am open to unexpected opportunities." — Sweet Potato Pasta with Alfredo Sauce   175

Veggie Curry

That thing that's getting in your way, those habits that are holding you back, that relationship that hasn't felt aligned in a while. LET. IT. ALL. GO. It's as simple as making the choice to release everything that's not serving you. It took you weeks, years, maybe even a lifetime to manifest those patterns, so you can bet it might take time to release them. This dish is both nourishing and grounding, helping to center you so that you can move forward with conviction.

SHIPS SETTING SAIL VISUALIZATION

Sit comfortably with your eyes closed and palms facing up, and start taking long, deep breaths. Release any tension and allow yourself to center on your breath. Let any noise that might be lurking around your mind evaporate. Now, envision yourself sitting on the edge of a long dock, looking out onto a beautiful lake. To your left, you see several small wooden boats, no bigger than a man's shoe. Pick up a boat and set an intention for something you are ready to let go of. As you hold the boat in your hands, bring this intention to mind, inhale big, and as you exhale out, drop your boat into the lake and watch it float away. Repeat this for the rest of your boats, with each thing you are ready to release. When you are done, take a deep breath in and sit in the lightness of your being in this moment. Feel the relief from letting go all of what's holding you back. Exhale and relax.

Yield: 4 servings

INGREDIENTS

1 tablespoon (12 g) raw extra-virgin coconut oil
1 white onion, diced
1 clove garlic, finely chopped
1 tablespoon (6 g) fresh grated ginger
1 tablespoon (15 ml) curry powder
1 teaspoon ground cumin
1 teaspoon ground coriander
1 teaspoon ground turmeric
Pinch of ground cayenne pepper
½ cup (50 g) broccoli florets, diced
½ cup (50 g) cauliflower florets, diced
¼ cup (31 g) carrots, sliced
(2) 14-ounce (403 ml) cans light coconut milk
1 cup (240 ml) vegetable stock
¼ cup (25 g) snow peas, coarsely chopped
Sea salt and freshly ground black pepper, to taste
Chopped cilantro and scallion, for garnish (optional)
Warm naan bread, cooked quinoa, or steamed brown rice, to serve (optional)

1. Heat the oil in a large saucepan over medium heat. Add the onions and sauté for 5 minutes until softened, then add the garlic and sauté for another minute. Add the spices and stir for 2 to 3 minutes.

2. Add the broccoli, cauliflower, and carrots, and sauté for another 5 minutes. Pour in the coconut milk and vegetable stock, bring to a boil, reduce the heat, and simmer for 5 to 10 minutes. Add the snow peas and then simmer for another 5 minutes, until the vegetables are cooked through. Season with salt and pepper.

3. Transfer the curry to a bowl, garnish with cilantro and scallion, and serve with naan bread, quinoa, or brown rice.

"I release everything that is not serving me."

Mushroom Tacos

I am a big believer in new beginnings. Sometimes the darkest times in our lives—the breakdowns, the break-ups, the pain—leads to a rebirth, a magical new era of ourselves. Beginnings can come in all sizes, whether they're as big as moving to start over or as seemingly small as deciding to begin a morning meditation practice. So forget about what you are leaving behind and focus your attention on what you are ready to create moving forward. I love this dish because it feels a bit like the anti-taco or a whole new experience of a taco.

SETTING INTENTIONS VISUALIZATION

Sit in a comfortable seated position with your palms facing up on your knees and your eyes closed. Take a few deep breaths and see yourself at the edge of a lake, sitting on the sand or rocks surrounding you and looking out onto the beautiful water. Notice a small pile of seeds to your right. Pick up a seed and hold it in your hand. Set an intention for a new beginning, to create something in your life, and once you set it, see and feel what it looks like coming to life. When you are ready, dig a small hole in front of you and plant it. Repeat this with as many seeds and intentions as you like. When you are complete, place both of your hands over the newly planted dirt and infuse it with love. Allow yourself to feel supported, knowing that your seeds are on their way to sprouting. Sit back and allow for the universe to work its natural magic. Take a deep breath in and hold it, fill yourself up with all the gratitude and excitement for all these intentions coming to life, and then exhale.

Yield: 4 tacos

INGREDIENTS
Olive oil cooking spray, for greasing
6 new potatoes, diced
Sea salt, to taste
2 tablespoons (30 ml) extra-virgin olive oil
½ white onion, quartered
1 clove garlic, chopped
¾ cup (53 g) cremini mushrooms
¾ cup (65 g) oyster mushrooms
¾ cup (48 g) enoki mushrooms
4 corn tortillas (or gluten-free taco shells)
4 romaine lettuce leaves, roughly chopped

SAUCE
1 avocado, halved and pitted
2 or 3 sprigs cilantro
2 tablespoons (30 g) grated horseradish
2 tablespoons (28 g) vegan sour cream

1. Preheat the oven to 425°F (220°C, or gas mark 7).

2. Grease a medium baking sheet with cooking spray. Sprinkle the potatoes with salt and roast in the oven for 10 to 15 minutes, until they begin to brown.

3. Heat the oil in a large frying pan over medium heat. Add the onions and sauté for 3 minutes, or until softened, then add the garlic and sauté for another minute. Add the mushrooms and cook for 5 minutes.

4. To make the sauce, in a food processor, add the avocado, cilantro, horseradish, and sour cream and pulse until thick and creamy.

5. Place a tortilla in a dry frying pan over medium heat and cook for about 45 seconds on each side, until warm and lightly brown. Repeat with the remaining tortillas.

6. To plate, lay out the warm tortillas. Place the chopped lettuce in the center, top with the mushroom mixture and roasted potatoes, and drizzle with the tangy avocado cream sauce. Enjoy!

△ "I welcome a new beginning."

Cauliflower Fried Rice

In the metaphysical text *A Course in Miracles*, it refers to a miracle as simply a shift in perception. And I can tell you from experience that I have welcomed some incredible miracles into my life just from uttering the words in the "Asking for a Miracle" meditation below. This dish is a great example of seeing things differently. Fried rice doesn't have to be made with rice at all. Here, I turned cauliflower into "rice" in my food processor. Also, it's absolutely delicious.

ASKING FOR A MIRACLE

Close your eyes, if possible. Put your hands on your heart, and bring to the top of your mind the situation for which you are asking for a miracle. Once you have it, simply say, "I surrender this situation. I am willing to see things differently. I am ready for a miracle. Thank you." Take a deep breath in and feel that miracle on its way and then exhale. Relax and go about your day. If the situation pops up again throughout the day, simply repeat, "I surrender this situation. I am willing to see things differently." Expect miracles!

Yield: 2 servings

INGREDIENTS

1 head cauliflower, florets separated and
   coarsely chopped
1 tablespoon (15 ml) sesame oil
1 yellow onion, diced
1 clove garlic, chopped
2 cups (170 g) broccoli slaw (with cabbage
   and carrots)
2 tablespoons (18 g) sesame seeds
½ cup (50 g) chopped scallions

SAUCE

¼ cup (80 ml) tamari (gluten-free soy sauce)
2-inch (5 cm) piece ginger root, finely chopped
   (use less if you are not a huge fan of ginger)
1 tablespoon (15 ml) onion powder

1. Place the cauliflower in a food processor and pulse until rice-like in appearance. Set aside.

2. Heat the sesame oil in a large frying pan over medium heat, add the onion, garlic, and broccoli slaw, and sauté for 2 minutes.

3. To make the sauce, combine the ingredients in a small bowl and mix well.

4. Stir the cauliflower rice into the broccoli-slaw mixture, and then add the sesame seeds and sauce. Cook for another 5 minutes, and then transfer into individual serving bowls and top with the chopped scallions.

"I am willing to see things differently."

Grandma's Galumpkis (Stuffed Cabbage Rolls)

One of the first things I remember learning from my grandma was "don't sweat the small stuff . . . and it's all small stuff." I have discovered that we have two options when handling a challenging situation: we can become hysterical and be the victim (I'm totally guilty of this) or we can take a deep breath, remain calm, and push forward with courage and grace to the next step. I thought it would be fun to recreate a dish from my grandma's childhood. She told me about these "galumpkis" she used to love when she was growing up. They are normally filled with rice and chopped meat, but this recipe calls for filling them with vegetables, lentils, and rice.

KUNDALINI MEDITATION FOR AEROBIC CAPACITY AND EFFICIENCY

Sit in easy pose with your palms face down on your knees. Inhale completely with a long, deep breath. Stretch your rib cage to its maximum capacity. Suspend the breath by lifting the chest and diaphragm. Do not let any air leak in or out during the exercise. Lock your tongue on the roof of your mouth. Press your tongue up, behind the teeth and the most forward point of the roof of your mouth. Begin to flex the spine forward and backward as you hold on to your knees. Flex with a smooth, fairly rapid pace. (Focus on the full flex of the spine, trying not to hunch your shoulders forward.) When you can no longer hold the breath in comfortably, sit up straight and exhale forcefully. Quickly inhale and continue to flex the spine—continue for 11 minutes. To close the meditation, sit up straight and inhale deeply. Hold this final breath and concentrate on your third-eye point (the space between your eyebrows). Relax.

Yield: 4 servings

INGREDIENTS
Coconut oil cooking spray, for greasing
2 Japanese eggplants, halved

SAUCE
2 tablespoons (30 ml) extra-virgin olive oil
1 clove garlic, finely chopped
(2) 28-ounce (794 g) cans crushed tomatoes
2 tablespoons (30 ml) apple cider vinegar
2 teaspoons onion powder
2 teaspoons oregano
2 teaspoons basil
½ teaspoon salt
½ teaspoon pepper

(continued on page 162)

"I handle all situations with grace and courage."

FILLING

2 tablespoons (30 ml) extra-virgin olive oil

1 yellow onion, diced

1 clove garlic, finely chopped

2 tablespoons (8 g) finely chopped fresh parsley

2 tablespoons (32 g) tomato paste

2 cups (400 g) cooked green lentils

1½ cups (293 g) cooked brown rice

Salt and freshly ground black pepper, to taste

2 large heads cabbage, halved and core removed

1. Preheat the oven to 375°F (190°C, or gas mark 5). Lightly grease a medium baking sheet with cooking spray and set aside.

2. Slice the eggplants vertically and then lay the slices between layers of paper towels to draw out moisture. Place the eggplants on the prepared baking sheet and roast for 15 minutes, or until they begin to brown. Set aside but leave the oven on (to bake the cabbage rolls).

3. To make the sauce, heat the olive oil in a large saucepan over medium heat, add the garlic, and sauté for 1 to 2 minutes. Add the crushed tomatoes, apple cider vinegar, onion powder, oregano, basil, salt, and pepper. Bring to a boil, reduce the heat, and simmer for 5 minutes. Set aside.

4. To make the filling, heat the olive oil in another large saucepan over medium heat.

Add the onions and sauté for 5 minutes, until softened, then add the garlic and sauté for another minute. Add the roasted eggplant, parsley, tomato paste, ½ cup (125 g) sauce, lentils, and brown rice and mix until thoroughly combined. Season with salt and pepper to taste. Remove from the heat and transfer the mixture to a bowl.

5. Fill a small bowl with cold water and set aside. Fill a large saucepan halfway with water and bring to a boil over high heat. Gently pull apart each leaf of cabbage, blanch in the boiling water for 1 to 2 minutes or until pliable, and then use a slotted spoon to transfer the cabbage leaves into the bowl of cold water.

6. Line the bottom of a 9 x 13-inch (23 x 33 cm) baking dish (or two 9-inch, or 23 cm, round pans) with broken or less attractive leaves until entirely covered. Put a cabbage leaf on a clean work surface and place a teaspoon to a tablespoon of filling in the center of the leaf. Roll up the leaf, tucking the sides in, to create a little package. Place the roll, seam side down, in your dish. Continue with the remaining leaves and filling.

7. Pour the remaining sauce over the rolls and bake for 30 minutes, or until the leaves lining the dish begin to brown. Serve.

Spaghetti Squash with Fresh Herbs

Sometimes we get so caught up in the chaos of our lives that we tend to let our vision get foggy. It's time to pare down and let go of the white noise so that you can focus on what counts and get back in the flow. This dish is a wonderful example of how delicious things are just as they are. Fresh herbs are excellent for activating your clarity of mind, while the spaghetti squash is naturally grounding, allowing you to be both centered and clear at once.

LET GO MEDITATION

Set a timer for 5, 11, or 22 minutes, depending on how long you would like to meditate. I recommend at least 11 minutes, working your way up to 22 minutes. Sit in easy pose, close your eyes, and place your palms facing up on your knees, with your fingers in gyan mudra, and start taking long, deep breaths. Let your breath calm and restore you. Slowly incorporate the mantra "let go" by silently saying "let" on the inhale and "go" on the exhale. Allow space for a breath at the end of each mantra for you to really dive into and get lost in the mantra. Allow yourself to only focus on the mantra, not on what you need to let go. When the timer sounds, gently release the mantra and bring your focus back to your breath.

"I receive clarity through simplicity."

Yield: 2 servings

INGREDIENTS
1 spaghetti squash
2 tablespoons (30 ml) extra-virgin olive oil, divided
1 bulb roasted garlic (see step 3 of Best Veggie Burger Ever and Avocado Fries, page 169), chopped
1 tablespoon (2 g) chopped fresh rosemary
1 tablespoon (2 g) chopped fresh oregano
1 tablespoon (2 g) chopped fresh thyme
½ teaspoon salt

1. Preheat the oven to 425°F (220°C, or gas mark 7).

2. Using a fork, poke holes in the squash, place on a baking sheet, and roast on the middle rack for 45 minutes. Set aside and when cool enough to handle, slice it in half lengthwise. Scoop out the seeds and discard. Use a fork to scrape out the "spaghetti" strings and transfer to a bowl.

3. Heat 1 tablespoon (15 ml) olive oil in a frying pan over medium heat, add the chopped garlic, and cook for a few minutes until browned. Stir in the "spaghetti" and cook for another 2 to 3 minutes, then add the fresh chopped herbs.

4. Drizzle in the remaining 1 tablespoon (15 ml) olive oil and season with the salt. Toss briefly, then transfer to a bowl and serve.

Mexican Quinoa Avocado Boats

Have you ever felt hungry and at the same time had the divine realization that it was for something other than food? Our soul is trying to speak to us in those moments; it wants nourishment, but it needs something much richer than that slice of chocolate cake or that late-night pizza. It desires PASSION. What are you truly desiring when you start to feel hungry? What could you incorporate into your life that would provide *real* nourishment? These fun avocado boats will leave you feeling satisfied and nourished!

MEDITATION FOR SOUL NOURISHMENT

Find a comfortable spot in your home and lay a few special things in front of you. I recommend a candle, perhaps a picture or two of someone who inspires you or an angel, guru, guide of your preference, and any precious trinkets. Doing this sets the tone for a special moment with yourself and holds the space for you to hear what your intuition wants to tell you as clearly as possible. Have a notebook or a few sheets of paper on hand for afterward, as you may want to take a few minutes to write what has come up for you.

   Sit in a comfortable seated position with your palms facing up on your knees and your spine held straight and elongated. Take a deep breath in and feel your body relax and your heart space expand with each new breath. Notice the innate sense of love and support you have right inside just from focusing your attention to this area in the center of your chest. Allow yourself to sit in it for a little while. When you are ready, ask from deep within what nourishment you need. Ask where in your life can you infuse more passion— where have you been neglecting your passions? Allow yourself to inquire for a moment or two, and then sit back in the silence. Return your focus to your heart center and just breathe, feeling the space and listening for what comes up for the next 3 to 5 minutes. To close the meditation, take a deep breath in with tremendous gratitude for the wisdom shared and exhale. Relax, then jot down any revelations in your notebook. If nothing comes up for you, don't worry; you have opened up the question, so simply stay open for the day ahead and let yourself receive the guidance brought to you throughout the day!

Yield: 8 boats

INGREDIENTS

½ cup (85 g) uncooked quinoa, soaked in water
Pinch of salt
1 cup (240 ml) water
½ cup (97 g) precooked black beans, soaked in water
½ yellow pepper, chopped
½ red pepper, chopped
½ red onion, diced
¼ cup (4 g) chopped cilantro
¼ cup (60 ml) chile-infused macadamia nut oil or extra-virgin olive oil
Juice of ½ lime
4 avocados, halved and pitted

(continued on page 166)

1. Drain the quinoa, and then place in a medium saucepan along with a pinch of salt and the water. Bring to a boil, reduce the heat, and simmer for about 15 minutes, until cooked through and fluffy.

2. Meanwhile, drain the black beans and place them into a medium mixing bowl. Add the chopped peppers, red onion, and cilantro.

3. Add the cooked quinoa, oil, and lime juice to the mixing bowl and stir. Cut the avocados in half, remove the seed, and scoop in the quinoa mixture. *Voilà*—simple, fun and totally adorable healthy meal.

Note: If you're bringing these to a barbecue or leaving them out at a dinner, drizzle extra lime juice over the avocado to prevent it from browning.

"I am nourished by my passion."

Best Veggie Burger Ever and Avocado Fries

Our perfectionism paralyzes us. I repeat, our perfectionism paralyzes us. What areas of your life are you obsessed with making perfect? Now take a closer look: how does that need for everything to be just right stop you from fully expressing yourself? You don't have to wait until you've figured out your whole life to open the door to love. Life is messy and being imperfect is just part of the experience! This was one of those recipes that I had to step away from and come back to on a different day. When I did come back to it, I released all expectations, picked a completely different set of ingredients, and just set the intention to have fun. Of course, it turned out to be the best thing I've ever tasted!

KUNDALINI MEDITATION TO CHANGE THE EGO

Sit in easy pose. Lift your chest slightly and relax your arms down to your sides. Raise your hands to your heart center, and curl your fingers into loose fists with your thumbs pointing up. Touch the sides of the top of your thumbs together and allow the rest of your hands to stay separated. Focus your eyes on your thumbs' knuckles and narrow your eyelids. Bring your concentration to your breath and create a steady breath rhythm with the following ratio and pathway: Inhale through the nose slowly for about 8 seconds. Hold in the breath for about 8 seconds. Release the breath through the nose for 8 equal strokes. Hold the breath for 8 seconds. Continue for 3 minutes. End the meditation by inhaling deeply and stretching your hands over your head, opening and closing your fists several times. Relax the breath.

"I release the need to be perfect."

Yield: 12 burgers

INGREDIENTS

FLAX "EGG"
1 tablespoon (9 g) flaxseed meal
3 tablespoons (45 ml) water

BURGERS
Olive oil cooking spray, for greasing
1 bulb garlic, cloves separated and peeled
1 cup (164 g) cooked chickpeas
½ cup (35 g) cremini mushrooms
⅓ cup (80 g) Dijon mustard
1 tablespoon (15 ml) extra-virgin olive oil
2 teaspoons dried oregano
1 teaspoon ground turmeric
1 teaspoon onion powder
1 teaspoon salt
½ teaspoon black pepper
1 cup (200 g) cooked green lentils
1 cup (186 g) cooked quinoa (or "super grain" blend of quinoa, millet, and buckwheat)
½ cup (56 g) quinoa flour
12 gluten-free rolls, to serve
Baby kale, to serve
Sliced red onions, to serve

(continued on page 169)

SAUCE

3 tablespoons (45 g) eggless mayonnaise

1 tablespoon (16 g) tomato paste

1 teaspoon grated fresh horseradish

AVOCADO FRIES

Coconut oil, for greasing

2 tablespoons (30 ml) extra-virgin olive oil

2 tablespoons (18 g) flaxseed meal

6 tablespoons (90 ml) water

1 cup (60 g) panko bread crumbs

1 teaspoon onion powder

1 teaspoon salt, plus extra to taste

Freshly ground black pepper, to taste

1 teaspoon garlic powder

2 near-ripe avocados, halved and pitted

1. To make the flax "egg," mix together the flaxseed and water in a small bowl and set aside for 5 minutes, until thickened. Set aside.

2. To make the burgers, preheat the oven to 375°F (190°C, or gas mark 5). Lightly grease a baking sheet with the cooking spray. Set aside.

3. Wrap the peeled garlic cloves in a small piece of foil, and place them in the oven for 20 minutes to roast.

4. In a food processor, combine the flax "egg," chickpeas, mushrooms, mustard, olive oil, spices, and roasted garlic, and pulse together until thoroughly combined. Transfer the mixture to a medium mixing bowl and add the lentils and quinoa. Using a spoon or your hands, thoroughly combine the mixture and gradually add the quinoa flour, a little at a time, until the mixture is thickened, but still moist.

5. Shape a heaping spoonful of the mixture into a ball, just slightly bigger than a golf ball. Place it onto the prepared baking sheet and flatten it out into a patty. Repeat with the remaining mixture (you should have about a dozen burgers—I always freeze at least half and keep some in the fridge for later in the week). Bake for 20 minutes, or until the outer edges lose their moisture and appear on the drier side.

6. To make the sauce, combine all the ingredients together and mix well.

7. Separate a gluten-free bun and place on a plate. Put a patty on one side, top with a generous slathering of sauce, baby kale, and red onion slices.

8. To make the fries, preheat the oven to 425°F (220°C, or gas mark 7). Lightly grease a baking sheet with coconut oil. In one bowl, whisk together the flaxseed meal and water. In another bowl mix your panko and seasonings. Slice the avocados lengthwise, dip in the flaxseed mixture, and then into the panko mixture.

9. Place on the prepared baking sheet and adjust the seasoning to taste. I like to add a couple more shakes of garlic and onion powder and a little more salt before they go in the oven. Bake for 10 minutes, or until the panko starts to brown. Any extra sauce can be used for dipping!

Lentil Shepherd's Pie

"What if everything in your life was happening for you and it was all designed to get you where you wanted to go?" I heard this quote five years ago on a YouTube video and it literally changed my life. I keep this quote close to my heart to this day, and now looking back, I can see exactly how my life during that time—struggles and all—was exactly where I needed it to be in order to be in the wonderful place I am today. Who doesn't love a nice hearty dish, especially in the winter, that makes you feel like you are wrapped in a blanket? I like making this dish for friends on a Sunday and eating the leftovers all week for lunch.

KUNDALINI MEDITATION FOR PERSPECTIVE AND EMOTIONAL BALANCE (ALTERNATE NOSTRIL BREATHING)

Sit in easy pose with your eyes closed, focusing on your third-eye point (the space between your eyebrows). Use your right thumb and right pinkie to close off alternate nostrils (you can also use the thumb and index finger). Close off the right nostril with your thumb. Inhale deeply through the left nostril. When the breath is full, close off the left nostril with your pinkie and exhale smoothly through the right nostril. The breath should be complete, continuous, and smooth. Continue for 3 minutes, gradually building up to 31 minutes. Close with a deep inhale, then exhale, holding the breath out and applying root lock by tensing your rectum and sex organs. Relax.

Yield: 8 servings

INGREDIENTS

FILLING

2 tablespoons (30 ml) extra-virgin olive oil

1 white onion, diced

1 clove garlic

1½ cups (264 g) dried green lentils

4 cups (960 ml) mushroom stock

3 sprigs of rosemary, plus extra to garnish

Coconut oil cooking spray, for greasing

½ cup (61 g) thinly sliced and halved carrots

½ cup (73 g) peas

½ cup (34 g) baby kale

¼ cup (41 g) corn kernels

2 tablespoons (30 ml) arrowroot powder (optional)

Salt, to taste

TOPPING

2 tablespoons (30 ml) extra-virgin olive oil

5 Yukon gold potatoes, peeled and sliced

Salt, to taste

1 white onion, diced

1 clove garlic, chopped

¼ cup (56 g) vegan butter

¼ cup (60 g) unsweetened almond milk

Freshly ground black pepper, to taste

1. To make the filling, heat the oil in a large frying pan over medium heat. Add the onions and sauté for 5 minutes until softened, then add the garlic and sauté for another minute. Add the lentils, mushroom stock, and rosemary. Bring to a gentle boil, then reduce the heat and simmer for 35 minutes.

2. To make the topping, put the potatoes in a large saucepan, cover with water, and add salt. Bring to a gentle boil over medium-high heat, and then cover and cook for 20 minutes, or until the potatoes have softened. Drain the potatoes and set aside.

3. Heat the oil in a frying pan over medium heat. Add the onion and sauté for 5 minutes, until softened, then add the garlic and sauté for another minute.

4. Transfer the potatoes, onion mixture, vegan butter, and almond milk to a blender or food processor. Pulse until combined but don't over-purée. Season with salt and pepper.

5. Meanwhile, preheat the oven to 425°F (220°C, or gas mark 7). Lightly grease a round, 2-quart (2 L) baking dish.

6. Add the carrots, peas, baby kale, and corn to the frying pan of lentils and cook for another 5 to 10 minutes, until the carrots are tender. Add the arrowroot powder to thicken the mixture, if desired. Remove the sprigs of rosemary, season with salt, and transfer the mixture to the baking dish.

7. Scoop the mashed potato topping over the lentil mixture until it's entirely covered. Bake in the oven for 10 to 15 minutes, or until the potatoes start to brown. Garnish with chopped rosemary and serve!

△ *"I feel loved and supported."*

Brussels Sprout Tacos

Take the time today to fall in love with the little things. Savor each sweet moment and start paying attention to all the ways you find more enjoyment as you flow through your day. When I think about being in love with the little things in life, Brussels sprouts, avocados, and tacos come to my mind.

LOVING THE MOMENT MEDITATION

Sit in easy pose and close your eyes, with your hands in gyan mudra. Relax your face, lengthen your spine, and start breathing, long and deep, in through your nose and out your mouth. Focus your attention at your heart center and feel a glowing ball of light expanding with each breath. Bring to mind a time when you felt in love with life. Allow that feeling to permeate your entire being, growing more and more potent with each breath as the light from your heart center grows to cover your entire being. Sit in this golden ball of light and love energy, soak it in for as long as you like, and then start to bring your practice to a close by returning your focus to your breathing and gently bringing yourself back into the room. Know that you can take that feeling with you wherever you go and call upon it in any moment when you want to be reminded of your natural state of being as love.

Yield: 4 tacos

INGREDIENTS

½ cup (44 g) chopped Brussels sprouts
1 tablespoon (15 g) Dijon mustard or horseradish
½ teaspoon garlic powder
½ teaspoon onion powder
Salt and freshly ground black pepper, to taste
Coconut oil cooking spray, for greasing

4 to 6 slices (¼ inch, or 6 mm, thick) tempeh or extra-firm tofu, cut into bite-sized pieces (you can substitute with black beans)
3 tablespoons (45 ml) organic barbecue sauce or garlic teriyaki sauce
4 flour tortillas (or corn for gluten-free)
2 romaine lettuce leaves, shredded
1 medium carrot, shredded
1 avocado, halved, pitted, and sliced
1 shallot, thinly sliced

1. In a medium bowl, combine the Brussels sprouts, Dijon or horseradish, garlic powder, onion powder, and a little salt and pepper and mix well until the Brussels sprouts are thoroughly coated.

2. Spray a little cooking spray on a medium frying pan and gently sauté the Brussels sprouts for 5 to 7 minutes, or until lightly browned. Set aside.

3. Heat the tempeh or tofu in a nonstick frying pan over medium heat and add the barbecue or garlic teriyaki sauce. Stir for 5 minutes, or until heated through and slightly crisp.

4. Place a tortilla in a dry frying pan over medium heat and cook for about 45 seconds on each side, until warm and lightly brown. Repeat with the remaining tortillas.

5. Place the lettuce in the center of a tortilla, and then add the carrots, Brussels sprouts, and tempeh or tofu. Top with slices of avocado and shallots, and then wrap closed.

"I am in love with the little things."

Sweet Potato Pasta with Alfredo Sauce

Sometimes we get so fixed on an idea of something that we close ourselves off from the infinite amount of possibilities for how it could manifest in our lives. I encourage you to think about something you deeply desire right now and strip it down to its basic core, releasing all of its trappings. When we are clear about what we truly desire, we open the door to unexpected opportunities and keep our eyes open for them along the way. Expand your options and expect miracles. Talk about an unexpected way to get your cravings met! If you have been craving the warm, filling, creamy decadence of fettuccine Alfredo without the dairy and gluten, then this is the recipe for you.

FEELING IT MEDITATION

Sit in easy pose with your hands over your heart, eyes closed, breathing in through your nose and out your mouth. Allow yourself to fill up from your heart radiating outward with the feelings of your desire fulfilled. Release any specific images that may come up and return to your heart and tune in to the feeling that is enveloping you around having what you truly desire. Sit in this feeling for the next 3 minutes. When time is up, take a deep breath in and silently say to yourself, "I release my attachment to what it looks like and I welcome in unexpected ways for it to manifest." Exhale and relax.

Yield: 2 servings

INGREDIENTS

SAUCE

15-ounce (425 g) can cannellini beans, drained and rinsed
15-ounce (425 g) can chickpeas, drained and rinsed
½ cup (120 ml) unsweetened almond milk
7 tablespoons (105 g) nutritional yeast
3 tablespoons (45 ml) extra-virgin olive oil
2 tablespoons (30 g) Dijon mustard
1 tablespoon (14 g) vegan butter
1 tablespoon (15 ml) garlic powder
1 tablespoon (15 ml) salt, plus extra to taste

½ teaspoon ground turmeric
2 tablespoons (30 ml) extra-virgin olive oil
2 sweet potatoes, skinned and spiralized
Chopped walnuts, to garnish
Chopped parsley, to garnish

1. To make the sauce, combine all the sauce ingredients in a food processor and pulse until thick and creamy. Season with salt to taste.

2. Heat the olive oil in a medium saucepan and sauté the sweet potato "noodles" for 5 minutes, until softened. Add the sauce to the saucepan and cook for 2 to 3 minutes, until heated through. Garnish with the walnuts and parsley, and serve. (Alternatively, heat the sauce in a separate saucepan and ladle it over a plate of noodles.)

"I am open to unexpected opportunities."

CHAPTER 11

Desserts

"I surrender my attachments." — Barely Baked Brownies   179

"My pure intentions radiate outward." — Vanilla Chai Cupcakes   180

"I speak sweetly to myself." — Chocolate Chip Hazelnut Heaven Cookies   183

"I treat myself divinely." — Chocolate "Caramel" Truffles   185

"I allow myself to relax and receive." — Lavender Tea Cookies   187

"I send love to those whom I find most difficult." — Cocoa Cupcakes   188

"I choose to lean on my soul." — Mini Carrot Cakes with Cashew Cream Cheese Frosting   190

"My authenticity is attractive." — Mixed Berry Tartlets   193

"I appreciate both the sweet and the sour in my life." — Key Lime Pie Bars   195

"I make space for adventure." — Mini Cheesecakes   196

Barely Baked Brownies

When we are attached to a particular outcome or person, we block ourselves from just being present in the moment. We miss the real opportunities because we are not able to show up completely as our authentic selves. Luckily, the opposite is also true: we become magnetic when we detach ourselves from expected outcomes and just allow ourselves to be present. Nothing reminds me more of the emotional disasters that have resulted from being too attached to something than indulging in a tray of brownies! Well, now you can eat these healthier brownies from a place of joy.

A MEDITATION TO RELEASE ATTACHMENTS

Sit comfortably in easy pose spine straight and your eyes closed. Take a few deep breaths and bring your focus inside your body. Now, envision the person or situation that you are currently attached to. See a long, thick rope all the way from your heart, wrapping around the person or situation. Next, welcome in an angel or a friend (if you prefer) and watch as they take a giant pair of scissors and cut the rope between you and your attachment. See the rope fall, your end no longer attached as it slowly begins to crumble into dust. Take a deep breath in and feel the energetic release. See your former attachment through love and newfound freedom. Take a deep breath in and hold it, locking in this feeling of relief and unattachment, and then exhale and relax. Repeat as often as necessary while you are working on releasing your attachments.

"I surrender my attachments."

Yield: 8 servings

INGREDIENTS

2 teaspoons flaxseed meal

2 tablespoons (30 ml) water

1 tablespoon (12 g) raw extra-virgin coconut oil, for greasing

1⅓ cups (182 g) gluten-free flour

1 cup (244 g) unsweetened applesauce

1 cup (160 g) vegan sugar-free chocolate chips

¾ cup (65 g) unsweetened cocoa powder

½ cup (120 ml) brown-rice syrup

1 teaspoon vanilla extract

½ teaspoon baking soda

Chopped walnuts, to garnish

Berries, to garnish

1. To make flax "egg," mix together the flaxseed and water in a small bowl and set aside for 5 minutes, until thickened.

2. Preheat the oven to 375°F (190°C, or gas mark 5) and grease an 8-inch (20 cm) baking dish with coconut oil.

3. In a medium mixing bowl, combine all of the remaining ingredients and flax "egg" until thoroughly mixed and pour the batter into the prepared baking dish. Bake for 15 to 20 minutes and then remove to cool. (Cook for less time if you really want them "barely baked.") Garnish with chopped walnuts or fresh berries.

Vanilla Chai Cupcakes

Are you in need of a shift in some area of your life? Let's say it's your romantic life. What if you purified your intentions to determine what you really want, which is probably more along the lines of experiencing joy by connecting to another person. The person who goes on a date with *that* intention is going to radiate joy and light that will be felt by others. Anchoring yourself in the pureness of your true intentions will shine in every area of your life. When I first started making cupcakes and was selling them at small fairs and pop-up shops, I didn't offer vanilla because I had more creative flavors. But kids would always want vanilla! And how could I not serve the kiddies? So I went into the kitchen and made these cupcakes with all the love in my heart.

A MEDITATION TO PURIFY INTENTIONS

Sit comfortably with your eyes closed and your palms facing up. Take a few long, deep breaths and center yourself in the quiet within you. Bring the troubled area of your life to the forefront. Look at the intention that's currently behind the wheel. See it for what it is, without any judgment. Now bring up these questions: What do I truly desire? How do I really want to operate in this area? Let your true intentions float to the surface and then sit in what should feel like a shift in your being. When you are ready, take a deep breath in, holding it and letting it soak into every cell of your being. Exhale.

Yield: 12 cupcakes

INGREDIENTS

CUPCAKES

2 cups (480 ml) unsweetened vanilla almond milk
2 teaspoons apple cider vinegar
2 chai tea bags
2 cups (224 g) quinoa flour
½ cup (77 g) date sugar
2 teaspoons baking powder
2 teaspoons baking soda
2 teaspoons ground cinnamon
2 teaspoons ground nutmeg
2 teaspoons ground cloves
1 teaspoon salt
½ cup (100 g) melted raw extra-virgin coconut oil
½ cup (120 ml) maple syrup
½ cup (122 g) unsweetened applesauce
1 tablespoon (15 ml) vanilla extract
1 teaspoon almond extract
1 cup (86 g) unsweetened coconut flakes,
    for decorating

"My pure intentions radiate outward."

ICING

1 cup (192 g) nonhydrogenated shortening

¼ cup (60 ml) coconut cream

¼ cup (60 ml) maple syrup or brown-rice syrup

3 tablespoons (48 g) cashew butter

2 teaspoons ground nutmeg

2 teaspoons ground cloves

2 teaspoons vanilla extract

2 teaspoons almond extract

1 teaspoon ground cinnamon

SPICE BLEND

½ teaspoon ground cinnamon

½ teaspoon ground nutmeg

½ teaspoon ground cloves

1. Preheat the oven to 375°F (190°C, or gas mark 5) and line a 12-cup muffin pan with paper baking cups.

2. To make the cupcakes, combine the almond milk and apple cider vinegar in a large measuring cup, stir, and then add the tea bags. Set it aside to steep (the mixture should curdle).

3. Meanwhile, combine all the dry ingredients together in a stand mixer or medium mixing bowl and mix well until clump-free. Add the coconut oil, maple syrup, applesauce, and extracts.

4. Remove the tea bags from the measuring cup and pour the curdled tea into the batter. Mix at medium-low speed (or by hand) until the ingredients are thoroughly combined. Using an ice-cream scooper or tablespoon, fill each cup three-quarters of the way with batter. Bake for 15 to 17 minutes, or until a toothpick inserted into the center of a cupcake comes out clean. Set aside to cool.

5. Meanwhile, make the icing. Combine all the ingredients in a bowl and whip at medium-high speed until fluffy and creamy. Ice the cupcakes and top with coconut flakes.

6. Combine the spice blend ingredients and sprinkle over the cupcakes.

Chocolate Chip Hazelnut Heaven Cookies

The quality of the conversation we have with ourselves on a daily basis has a major impact on our lives. It's pretty hard to be a positive, beaming person when your internal critic is constantly berating you. My antidote to this critical inner voice is to take notice and realize that it's not me or my truth. Then I laugh at how silly it is and readjust to thinking something positive. It takes a bit of practice to get into this habit, but it's a total game changer! When I first gave up dairy and gluten, I panicked thinking about a life without chocolate chip cookies. It just felt wrong and unfair, until one morning when I got a little more creative and made these delightful treats!

MEDITATION FOR SELF-KINDNESS

Sit in easy pose with your spine elongated and your eyes closed. Begin taking deep breaths in through your nose and out your mouth. Bring your focus to your heart center. Imagine a glowing ball of bright golden light right there in the center of your being. See it growing brighter and radiating more with each breath. Now allow yourself to bring to mind the things you genuinely love about yourself. What endearing things do you do? Let your mind wander and allow it to flood you with all the beautiful facets of you—big and small—that are magnificent. It's okay if you feel uncomfortable at first; we are not used to speaking to ourselves so sweetly so it can feel a little strange. Relax, allow, and receive. Bask in your heart's expanding glow and continue for 3 minutes. Then take a deep breath in and hold it, infusing every cell of your body with that sweet, tender, loving-kindness. Exhale.

Yield: 12 cookies

INGREDIENTS

2 teaspoons flaxseed meal
2 tablespoons (30 ml) water
3 tablespoons (36 g) raw extra-virgin coconut oil, divided
1½ cups (141 g) gluten-free oat bran
2 tablespoons (32 g) cashew, almond, or hazelnut butter (I prefer the creamy sweetness of cashew butter)
1 large banana
½ cup (58 g) sliced hazelnuts
2 teaspoons vanilla extract
1 teaspoon almond extract
1 teaspoon ground cinnamon
½ cup (80 g) vegan sugar-free chocolate chips

1. To make flax "egg," mix together the flaxseed and water in a small bowl and set aside for 5 minutes, until thickened.

2. Preheat the oven to 375°F (190°C, or gas mark 5) and grease a baking sheet with 1 tablespoon (12 g) coconut oil. Set aside.

3. In a stand mixer, combine the oat bran, cashew butter, remaining 2 tablespoons (24 g) coconut oil, banana, hazelnuts, vanilla extract, almond extract, cinnamon, and flax "egg" and mix on medium speed until thoroughly combined. Add the chocolate chips and mix on low speed. Using an ice-cream scooper or a tablespoon, scoop and place the cookie dough on the baking sheet, about 2 inches (5 cm) apart. Bake for 10 to 12 minutes, or until the tops begin to dry.

"I speak sweetly to myself."

ICING

1½ cups (195 g) cashew nuts, soaked in water for
    2 to 3 hours and then drained

¼ cup (60 ml) canned coconut milk

¼ cup (22 g) unsweetened coconut flakes

4 teaspoons vanilla extract

Juice of 1 lemon

10 drops vanilla stevia

GARNISH

Pinch of ground cinnamon

Chopped walnuts, to taste

1. Preheat your oven to 375°F (190°C, or gas
   mark 5) and grease a 12-cup muffin pan with
   coconut oil or line with paper baking cups.

2. To make the cake, first make flax "egg."
   Mix together the flaxseed and water in a
   small bowl and set aside for 5 minutes, until
   thickened.

3. Combine the almond milk and apple cider
   vinegar in a large measuring cup, stir, and set
   aside to curdle.

4. Combine the remaining cake ingredients in a
   food processor and pulse to combine. Add in
   the flax "egg" and almond milk mixture and
   purée until the consistency is like cake batter.
   Pour the mixture into your muffin cups, filling
   them halfway (and keeping the top flat for
   the icing). Bake for 15 minutes, or until a
   toothpick inserted into the center of the cake
   comes out clean. Set aside to cool.

5. To make the icing, combine all ingredients in a
   food processor or blender and mix well. Place
   the icing in the refrigerator to chill while the
   cakes are cooling. Give the icing a good stir
   before icing the cupcakes.

6. To garnish, sprinkle over the cinnamon and
   top with the walnuts.

Mixed Berry Tartlets

There is divine magic in sharing our authentic selves, because when we do, we make others feel more comfortable being themselves as well. There is nothing more attractive than being unapologetically you. When we put on an act, we can sever connections with others because we become unrelatable. Your authenticity will make you magnetic! I love how true this tart is in representing the natural flavors of the berries. I specifically kept all of the spices in the crust so the fruit can really stand alone.

KUNDALINI SELF-CARE BREATH KRIYA

Sit comfortably in easy pose or another meditation posture. Open your mouth and form a circle with it that is tight and precise. Place your hands at your heart center, right over left. Close your eyes and sense the area under your palms. Breathe a steady, powerful breath through the mouth. Let your mind focus on the ring of your mouth and shape the breath into a ring. Continue for 5 minutes. To end the meditation, inhale and hold the breath. Relax the mouth. Mentally repeat, "I am beautiful, I am innocent, I am innocent, I am beautiful." Exhale through the nose. Do this a total of 5 times and then relax.

Yield: Makes 12 tartlets

INGREDIENTS

1 tablespoon (14 g) vegan butter, melted, for greasing

CRUST

1½ cups (204 g) gluten-free flour blend
3 tablespoons (29 g) date sugar
1 tablespoon (15 ml) ground cinnamon
2 teaspoon ground nutmeg
1 teaspoon almond extract
¼ cup (56 g) soy-free vegan butter, chilled
3 tablespoons (36 g) raw extra-virgin coconut oil
1 tablespoon (15 ml) apple cider vinegar
¼ cup (60 ml) cold water

FILLING

1 cup (166 g) fresh or frozen strawberries, chopped
1 cup (150 g) fresh or frozen blueberries
1 cup (144 g) fresh or frozen blackberries
1 tablespoon (15 ml) vanilla extract
Maple syrup (optional)

GARNISH

¼ cup (25 g) crushed walnuts
¼ cup (18 g) almond slivers
¼ cup (22 g) unsweetened coconut flakes

1. Preheat the oven to 375°F (190°C, or gas mark 5) and lightly grease a 12-cup muffin pan.

2. To make the crust, combine all the ingredients in a food processor and pulse until a dough is formed. Roll a small amount of the mixture into a 2-inch (5 cm) ball with and spread it out to line the muffin cup. Use a fork to lightly press the tines into the pastry. Repeat with the rest of the dough, and then bake for 15 minutes or until golden.

3. Meanwhile, make the filling. Combine the berries in a small bowl and add vanilla extract and maple syrup to sweeten, if desired. Scoop a few tablespoons into each cup and bake for another 10 to 15 minutes, or until the edges start to brown.

4. Garnish with the walnuts, almonds, and coconut flakes!

"My authenticity is attractive."

Key Lime Pie Bars

We may think we want the sweet parts of our lives all the time—the happiness, excitement, and success—but what we don't often account for is how the not-so-sweet times help us to really appreciate the sweet times. As writer Kahlil Gibran says: "The deeper that sorrow carves into your being, the more joy you can contain." So wherever you are on the sweet-to-sour spectrum right now, sit in it, and embrace it. And what could be a more perfect example of how just enough sour with just enough sweet can make a really delicious combination than Key lime pie?

KUNDALINI MEDITATION FOR MATURITY AND WISDOM

Sit in easy pose. Bend your elbows down by your sides. Extend the forearms up so your hands are a few inches in front of each shoulder, palms flat and facing the body. Bend the palms back slightly at the wrists, until they are facing up, somewhat relaxed and lightly cupped. Hold this position. Without using the breath in any specific way, begin to pump the navel point powerfully. Pump very hard and very fast. Stare at the tip of your nose. Do this meditation for 3 minutes, gradually working your way up to 31 minutes. To end the meditation, inhale and pump the navel (pulling in your navel to the back of your spine and releasing) vigorously. Hold for 10 seconds. Exhale. Repeat for a total of 3 times. Relax.

Yield: 12 bars

INGREDIENTS

CRUST
1¼ cups (124 g) whole pecans
2 tablespoons (32 g) cashew butter
1 cup (175 g) pitted dates
1 tablespoon (12 g) raw extra-virgin coconut oil, for greasing

FILLING
1½ cups (195 g) raw unsalted cashew nuts, soaked in water for 2 to 3 hours and then drained
1 ripe avocado, halved, pitted, and sliced
⅔ cup (155 ml) Key lime juice (about 6 Key limes; you can substitute with 6 regular limes and 3 tablespoons, or 45 ml, cassava sweetener added to the juice, or omit it if you prefer a tart pie)

GARNISH
Zest of 2 Key limes

1. To make the crust, combine the pecans, cashew butter and dates in a food processor and pulse until thoroughly combined and clumpy. Grease a 12-cup muffin tray with coconut oil and then lay down the crust mix inside each cup, until 1 inch (2.5 cm) deep. Place the tray, flat, in the freezer while preparing the filling.

2. Meanwhile, make the filling. Clean the food processor, then add the avocado, cashews, and lime juice to the processor and pulse until a nice creamy mixture is created.

3. Remove the pan from the freezer and scoop about 2 tablespoons (30 g) filling into each cup. Garnish with the lime zest and a pecan and serve.

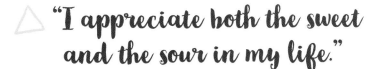
"I appreciate both the sweet and the sour in my life."

Mini Cheesecakes

Going on an adventure can be as simple as taking a new route home or trying a fruit you've never had before. Our bodies and souls crave adventure and variety, so when we get stuck in a monotonous routine, we can start feeling depressed. I like to create adventure in my life in the kitchen! These cheesecakes were a product of that desire. I was tempted to make something for dessert that I had never made before.

MYSTICAL ADVENTURE VISUALIZATION

Find a comfortable spot where you can relax. Close your eyes and focus on your third-eye point (the space between your eyebrows). Take long, deep, breaths, inhaling through your nose, deep into your diaphragm, and exhaling out your mouth. Bring to mind a place you would love to visit—whatever first comes to mind for you is perfect. Spend the next 11 minutes allowing yourself to explore that environment; wander around and have an experience. Allow any images that come up to be perfect and surrender to the journey. To end the meditation, take a deep breath in, come back to the room, then exhale. Rub your arms and legs with your hands to bring you back to earth.

Yield: 12 mini cakes

INGREDIENTS

CRUST
1 cup (175 g) pitted dates
3 tablespoons (19 g) chopped almonds
3 tablespoons (19 g) chopped walnuts
3 tablespoons (19 g) chopped hazelnuts
1 tablespoon (9 g) chia seeds
1 tablespoon (5 g) unsweetened cocoa powder
2 teaspoons vanilla extract
½ teaspoon ground cardamom

FILLING
1½ cups (195 g) raw unsalted cashew nuts, soaked in water for 2 to 3 hours and drained
Juice of 1 lemon
⅓ cup (66 g) raw extra-virgin coconut oil
½ cup (119 ml) canned coconut milk
1 tablespoon (15 ml) vanilla extract
2 teaspoons almond extract
Raspberries or cacao nibs and almond butter, to garnish (optional)

1. Line a 12-cup muffin pan with paper baking cups. To make the crust, combine all the ingredients in a food processor and pulse until well blended and clumpy. Roll a small amount of the mixture into a 2-inch (5 cm) ball and flatten it against the bottom of a muffin cup to form the crust for a cheesecake. Repeat with the remaining mixture, and then place the tray in the freezer.

2. Meanwhile, make the filling. Clean the food processor, add the filling ingredients, and purée until thick and creamy. Remove the pan from the freezer and pour the filling evenly into each cup, until each is about full. If desired, add a few raspberries or, alternatively, top with a dollop of almond butter and a few cacao nibs. Freeze for another 30 minutes, and then chill in the refrigerator until ready to serve!

 *"I make space for adventure."*

Index

Page references in *italics* indicate photographs.

A

A Living Meditation 116

AB&J Rice Cakes 87

Above the Battlefield Meditation 150

Addictions, Kundalini Meditation for 149

Aerobic Capacity and Efficiency, Kundalini
  Meditation for 161

Asian Broccoli Slaw 149

Asking for a Miracle 159

avocado:
  Avocado Black Bean Hash 90
  Avocado Toast Three Ways 82, *83*

B

balance 54
  Kundalini Meditation for Emotional
    Balance 123
  Meditation for Balancing the Nervous
    Energies 97

Barely Baked Brownies *178*, 179

Basic Breath 145

bath-time:
  Bath-Time Meditation 107
  I Am Divine Bath-Time Relaxation 185

being the lighthouse 51–52

Berry Green Smoothie 79

blueberries:
  Blueberry Almond Muffins 98, *99*
  Blueberry Basil Juice 69

Body Love Meditation 140

breakfast 80–109
  AB&J Rice Cakes 87
  Avocado Black Bean Hash 90
  Avocado Toast Three Ways 82, *83*
  Blueberry Almond Muffins 98, *99*
  Brunch Tacos 102, *103*, 104
  Cherry Rosemary Scones *100*, 101
  Chia Seed Pancakes 105
  Chia Seed Pudding 88, *89*
  Chilled Oatmeal 97
  Crack Bars *106*, 107, 108
  Creamy Cashew Yogurt *92*, 93
  Pumpkin Quinoa Pancakes *84*, 85, 86
  Quinoa Porridge 91
  Strawberry-Banana Gluten-Free Cakes 109
  Veggie Scramble with Turmeric Potatoes
    94, 95, 96

breathing:
  Basic Breath 145
  Kundalini Four-Stroke Breath to Build
    Intuition 105

Broken Heart, Meditation for a 109

Brownies, Barely Baked *178*, 179

Brunch Tacos 102, *103*, 104

Brussels sprout:
  Brussels Sprout Tacos 172, *173*
  Shaved Brussels Sprout Salad *132*, 133

building a foundation for expansion 39–40

Burger, Best Veggie Ever and Avocado Fries
  167, *168*, 169

Burnout, Meditation for 115

C

Caesar Salad 150, *151*

Caliber of Life Kundalini Meditation 71

California Kale Salad 137

Carrot Cakes with Cashew Cream Cheese
  Frosting, Mini 190, *191*, 192

Cashew Yogurt, Creamy *92*, 93

cauliflower:
  Cauliflower-Apple-Rosemary Soup *112*, 113, 114
  Cauliflower Fried Rice *158*, 159

change:
  integrating into your daily life 55–59
  Kundalini Meditation for Change 121
  Kundalini Meditation to Change the Ego 167

Cheesecakes, Mini 196

Cherry Rosemary Scones *100*, 101

chia seed:
  Chia Seed Pancakes 105
  Chia Seed Pudding 88, *89*

Chili, Veggie 128, *129*

Chilled Oatmeal 97

chocolate:

    Chocolate "Caramel" Truffles *184*, 185

    Chocolate Chip Hazelnut Heaven Cookies
      182, 183

Choosing Love Meditation 68

Cocoa Cupcakes 188, 189

cold turkey 45

Conquer Self-Animosity Kundalini
 Meditation 79

cookies:

    Chocolate Chip Hazelnut Heaven Cookies
      182, 183

    Lavender Tea Cookies *186*, 187

Crack Bars *106*, 107, 108

Crave Cure, the 27–28

Creamy Cashew Yogurt *92*, 93

Creamy Tomato Soup *122*, 123

cupcakes:

    Cocoa Cupcakes 188, 189

    Vanilla Chai Cupcakes 180, 181

Curry, Veggie 154, *155*

D

Deep-Healing Juice 76, *77*

desserts 176–196

    Barely Baked Brownies *178*, 179

    Chocolate "Caramel" Truffles *184*, 185

    Chocolate Chip Hazelnut Heaven Cookies
      182, 183

    Cocoa Cupcakes 188, 189

    Key Lime Pie Bars *194*, 195

    Lavender Tea Cookies *186*, 187

    Mini Carrot Cakes with Cashew
      Cream Cheese Frosting 190, *191*, 192

    Mini Cheesecakes 196

    Mixed Berry Tartlets 193

    Vanilla Chai Cupcakes 180, 181

Divine Purpose Visualization 62

Down to Earth Meditation 142

E

Earthy Juice *70*, 71

Easy Pose 13, *13*

eat with intention, meaning of 14–33

eating mindfully 32–33

Ego, Kundalini Meditation to Change the 167

Ego Eradicator 72

Emotional Balance, Kundalini Meditation for 123

emotional eating during stressful times 46–47

Energy, Kundalini Meditation for Absolutely
 Powerful 119

entrées 152–175

    Best Veggie Burger Ever and Avocado Fries 167,
      168, 169

    Brussels Sprout Tacos 172, *173*

    Cauliflower Fried Rice *158*, 159

    Grandma's Galumpkis (Stuffed Cabbage Rolls)
      160, 161–162

    Lentil Shepherd's Pie 170, 171

    Mexican Quinoa Avocado Boats *164*, 165, 166

    Mushroom Tacos 156, 157

    Spaghetti Squash with Fresh Herbs 163

    Sweet Potato Pasta with Alfredo Sauce
      174, 175

    Veggie Curry 154, *155*

F

Farmers' Market Juice *74*, 75

Feeling It Meditation 175

Focus Potion 62, *63*

Food-Mood Challenge, 2-Week 23–25

food-mood journal, start a 23

foundation for expansion, building a 39–40

G

Gazpacho, Watermelon 121

Grandma's Galumpkis (Stuffed Cabbage Rolls)
 160, 161–162

gratitude 18, 20

Green Lemonade 73

Grounding Salad 142, *143*, 144

H

habits, shifting your 42–47

Healing Light Meditation 76

Hillman, James 43

I

I Am Divine Bath-Time Relaxation 185

Increased Energy, Meditation for 95

Inner Conflict Resolver Reflex Meditation, Kundalini 127

Inner Rock Star Visualization 82

Interconnectedness Meditation 147

Intuition, Kundalini Four-Stroke Breath to Build 105

Intuitive Meditation and Writing Exercise 137

J

juices and smoothies 60–79

Berry Green Smoothie 79

Blueberry Basil Juice 69

Deep-Healing Juice 76, *77*

Earthy Juice *70*, 71

Farmers' Market Juice *74*, 75

Focus Potion 62, *63*

Green Lemonade 73

Radiance Juice *66*, 67

Standard Green Machine 72

Sunshine Juice 68

Unicorn Fuel *64*, 65

Watermelon Mint Juice 78

K

Key Lime Pie Bars *194*, 195

Know the Field Kundalini Meditation 65

Kundalini meditation 13

Addictions, for 149

Adi Shakti Mantra 187

Aerobic Capacity and Efficiency, for 161

Caliber of Life Meditation 71

Change, for 121

Conquer Self-Animosity Meditation 79

Ego, to Change the 167

Emotional Balance, for 123

Energy, for Absolutely Powerful 119

Four-Stroke Breath to Build Intuition 105

Inner Conflict Resolver Reflex Meditation 127

Know the Field Meditation 65

Mantra for Self-Esteem 138

Maturity and Wisdom, for 195

Negative Mind, for 113

Peace Begins With Me Meditation 135

Perspective and Emotional Balance, for (Alternate Nostril Breathing) 170

Self-Care Breath Kriya 193

Still the Mind Meditation 91

L

laughter:

healing nature of 53

spiritual nature of 21–22, 53

Lavender Tea Cookies *186*, 187

Leaning On Your Soul, Meditation for 190

Lemonade, Green 73

lentils:

Lentil Shepherd's Pie 170, 171

Lentil Veggie Soup *124*, 125

Let Go Meditation 93, 163

Light-Filled Meditation 90

lighthouse, being the 51–52

Loving the Moment Meditation 172

M

Make Your Own Gratitude Meditation 102

mantras:

Kundalini Adi Shakti Mantra 187

Kundalini Mantra for Self-Esteem 138

Maturity and Wisdom, Kundalini Meditation for 195

meal-planning miracle 47

meditation 9, 10, 11, 12, 18, 20, 25–27, 30, 32, 49, 50, 51–52, 53

A Living Meditation 116

Above the Battlefield Meditation 150

Balancing the Nervous Energies, for 97

Bath-Time Meditation 107

meditation (continued)

Body Love Meditation 140

Broken Heart, for a 109

Burnout, for 115

Caliber of Life Kundalini Meditation 71

Choosing Love Meditation 68

Conquer Self-Animosity Kundalini Meditation 79

daily 40–41

Down to Earth Meditation 142

Feeling It Meditation 175

Healing Light Meditation 76

Increased Energy, for 95

Interconnectedness Meditation 147

Intuitive Meditation and Writing Exercise 137

Know the Field Kundalini Meditation 65

Kundalini Inner Conflict Resolver Reflex Meditation 127

Kundalini Meditation for Absolutely Powerful Energy 119

Kundalini Meditation for Addictions 149

Kundalini Meditation for Aerobic Capacity and Efficiency 161

Kundalini Meditation for Change 121

Kundalini Meditation for Emotional Balance 123

Kundalini Meditation for Maturity and Wisdom 195

Kundalini Meditation for Perspective and Emotional Balance (Alternate Nostril Breathing) 170

Kundalini Meditation to Change the Ego 167

Leaning On Your Soul, for 190

Let Go Meditation 93, 163

Light-Filled Meditation 90

Loving the Moment Meditation 172

Make Your Own Gratitude Meditation 102

meditation 101 13

miracle moment, the 56–57

morning practice 55–56

new you, the 57, 59

Peace Begins with Me Kundalini Meditation 135

Positive Mind, for the 85

Purify Intentions, to 180

Radiant Heart Meditation 67

Release Attachments, to 179

Releasing, for *132*, 133

Seeing Innocence, for 125

Self-Forgiveness, for 126

Self-Kindness, for 183

Self-Love Meditation 88

Sending Love Meditation 188

Soul Nourishment, for 165

Still the Mind Kundalini Meditation 91

Sweet Moments Meditation 69

Synchronization Meditation 101

Walk in Nature Meditation 75

Waves of Abundance Meditation 87

well-being trifecta and 35, 37–39, 40–41

Mexican Quinoa Avocado Boats *164*, 165, 166

Mini Carrot Cakes with Cashew Cream Cheese Frosting 190, *191*, 192

Mini Cheesecakes 196

Mixed Berry Tartlets 193

mudra 13

Muffins, Blueberry Almond 98, *99*

mushrooms:

Mushroom Barley Soup 115

Mushroom Tacos 156, 157

My Ideal Day Visualization 128

Mystical Adventure Visualization 196

N

Negative Mind, Kundalini Meditation for the 113

negative self-talk, end 21, 22, 138

O

Oatmeal, Chilled 97

One-Size-Fits-All Nutrition 28

P

pancakes:

Chia Seed Pancakes 105

Pumpkin Quinoa Pancakes *84*, 85, 86

Pasta, Sweet Potato with Alfredo Sauce *174*, 175

Peace Begins With Me Kundalini Meditation 135

Perspective and Emotional Balance (Alternate Nostril Breathing), Kundalini Meditation for 170

Pillar 1: Making peace with your body 16–22

Pillar 2: Becoming a food detective 23–25

Pillar 3: Starting a conservation 25–28

Pillar 4: Fall In love with food 28–33

Porridge, Quinoa 91

Positive Mind, Meditation for the 85

Pranayam Energizer Series 73

Pudding, Chia Seed 88, *89*

Pumpkin Quinoa Pancakes *84*, 85, 86

Purify Intentions, a Meditation to 180

Q

quinoa:

Pumpkin Quinoa Pancakes *84*, 85, 86

Quinoa Porridge 91

R

Radiance Juice *66*, 67

Radiant Heart Meditation 67

Release Attachments, a Meditation to 179

releasing, meditation for *132*, 133

Rice Cakes, AB&J 87

Rooted Bowl, the *146*, 147, 148

S

Sacred Cooking 29–30

salads and bowls 130–151

Asian Broccoli Slaw 149

Caesar Salad 150, *151*

California Kale Salad 137

Grounding Salad 142, *143*, 144

Rooted Bowl, the *146*, 147, 148

Shaved Brussels Sprout Salad *132*, 133

Taco Salad with Chili-Lime Ranch Dressing *134*, 135, 136

Tofu Kale Waldorf Salad 140, 141

Tomato Arugula Salad 145

Yogi Bowl 138, *139*

Scones, Cherry Rosemary *100*, 101

Seeing Innocence, Meditation for 125

self-care 36, 49–51

self-care Sundays 50–51

Self-Care Breath Kriya, Kundalini 193

Self-Esteem, Kundalini Mantra for 138

Self-Forgiveness, a Mediation for 126

Self-Kindness, Meditation for 183

Self-Love Meditation 88

Sending Love Meditation 188

Setting Intentions Visualization 156

Shaved Brussels Sprout Salad *132*, 133

Ships Setting Sail Visualization 154

Sitali Pranayam (Cooling Breath) 78

situation triggers 45–46

Smoothie, Berry Green 79

Soul Nourishment, Meditation for 165

soups 110–128

Cauliflower-Apple-Rosemary Soup *112*, 113, 114

Creamy Tomato Soup *122*, 123

Lentil Veggie Soup *124*, 125

Mushroom Barley Soup 115

Spaghetti Squash Noodle Soup 116, *117*

Spicy Squash Soup 126

Spinach Artichoke Soup *118*, 119, 120

Veggie Chili 128, *129*

Veggie Tom Kha Gai 127

Watermelon Gazpacho 121

spaghetti squash:

Spaghetti Squash Noodle Soup 116, *117*

Spaghetti Squash with Fresh Herbs 163

Spicy Squash Soup 126

Spinach Artichoke Soup *118*, 119, 120

Standard Green Machine 72

Still the Mind Kundalini Meditation 91

Strawberry-Banana Gluten-Free Cakes 109

stop eating a food altogether 44–45

stress 46–47, 53–54

Sunshine Juice 68

Sweet Moments Meditation 69

Sweet Potato Pasta with Alfredo Sauce *174*, 175

Synchronization Meditation 101

T

tacos:

Brunch Tacos 102, *103*, 104

Brussels Sprout Tacos 172, *173*

Mushroom Tacos 156, 157

Taco Salad with Chili-Lime Ranch Dressing *134*, 135, 136

taking care of you 48–54

Tofu Kale Waldorf Salad 140, 141

tomatoes:

Creamy Tomato Soup *122*, 123

Tomato Arugula Salad 145

Transference, Visualization for 98

Truffles, Chocolate "Caramel" *184*, 185

Turmeric Potatoes, Veggie Scramble with *94*, 95, 96

2-Week Food-Mood Challenge 23–25

U

Unicorn Fuel *64*, 65

V

Vanilla Chai Cupcakes 180, 181

vegetables:

Veggie Chili 128, *129*

Veggie Curry 154, *155*

Veggie Scramble with Turmeric Potatoes *94*, 95, 96

Veggie Tom Kha Gai 127

visualization:

Divine Purpose Visualization 62

Inner Rock Star Visualization 82

My Ideal Day Visualization 128

Mystical Adventure Visualization 196

Setting Intentions Visualization 156

Ships Setting Sail Visualization 154

Visualization for Transference 98

W

Walk in Nature Meditation 75

watermelon:

Watermelon Gazpacho 121

Watermelon Mint Juice 78

Waves of Abundance Meditation 87

well-being trifecta 34–41

Writing Exercise, Intuitive Meditation and 137

Y

Yogi Bowl 138, *139*

Yogurt, Creamy Cashew *92*, 93

Acknowledgments

I would like to thank Jeannine Dillon and the entire Quarto family for taking a risk on something that was unlike any cookbook or lifestyle manual out there—for having faith in my vision of a world where people love their bodies, listen to their body's wisdom, and ultimately have a deeper connection with their soul. And, of course, for all their hard work in the creation and publication of this beautiful book. I have felt so loved, supported, and taken care of every step of the way and truly feel that all of that positive energy is infused in every page of this book from your end and mine.

I would like to thank Rossella Rago, the Veronica to my Betty in the kitchen and one of my dearest girlfriends, for passing along a note that I might be a great fit for a juice book, and for all the magic that ensued following that little flap of a butterfly's wings. This book wouldn't exist without your love and support, and I'm eternally grateful.

I would like to thank Mary Aracena, for being the best assistant, friend, recipe helper, and all-around support system during the creation of this book. I know I will fondly look back on those twelve-hour days we spent together laughing, crying, eating lots of food, and having minor breakdowns in the kitchen for the rest of my life. Your beautiful energy is infused in every corner of this book. You are truly a living angel in my life and I am incredibly grateful to have had you by my side during this magical time.

I would like to thank my parents, Ken and Debbie Bodzak, for having infinite amounts of patience with my always needing to take the road less traveled and often dancing to the beat of my own drummer. I am sure it hasn't been the easiest having me as a daughter, and you both have been so loving, supportive, and encouraging through it all. Thank you for cheering me on. Love you both tons. "Look, guys, I finally wrote the book!!" :)

Lastly, I would like to thank my grandma, Joan McDonald, for always being a steady rock in my life, an open ear, and a wise advisor. Your grace and courage in this life inspires me to constantly be a better version of myself, your patience and faith remind me to not sweat the small stuff (and it's all small stuff), and your love always feels like a bright ray of sunshine on my day. Love you madly.

Dedication

I dedicate this book to my brother, Kenneth Bodzak.

Kenny, I feel so privileged to be your sister in this life. It has always been a blessing to have a little brother that I felt was a teammate, someone I could share anything with, someone who always has my back, someone who would tell me the straight truth as well as lovingly make fun of me and laugh at my "woo woo" ways. Watching you handle the cards you have been dealt and facing the thought of losing you has done nothing short of transforming my life. I can wholeheartedly say I am not the woman I was when I first got that phone call from Mom. You have shown me what strength, courage, and fearlessness looks like in the face of terrifying circumstances, and yet you manage to keep a dark but rather hilarious sense of humor about the whole thing. You are my shining light, even when you are gloomy. I am so glad that we get to do this life together, and I can't wait for many more years to come. I love you more than I knew possible.

About the Author

Photo Credit: Mary Aracena

CASSANDRA BODZAK is a global meditation and wellness teacher who teaches people how to utilize the technologies of food, meditation, and self-care to make peace with their bodies and their plates, so that they can live their best life. Cassandra is an author, speaker, and certified kundalini yoga and meditation teacher. You may know her as the happy, healthy living guru from ABC's *The Taste* or the host of *Eat with Intention* TV as well as various other healthy online cooking series.

Dear Sweet Reader

You made it! And yet, you are only at the beginning of this glorious lifelong journey to love and honor your body, to navigate this wondrous world with your inner compass. Take all the tools you have learned here and keep them in your back pocket. Take the nuggets of wisdom that appeal to you and keep those close to your heart. Let yourself be a constant work in progress so the pitfalls don't paralyze you. Jump back on the horse and keep riding.

Every detour in life can show you a new side of yourself, strengthen your resolve, and require more grace from you if you let it. So fall in love with the windy road, the secret corners, and the sunlit, flower-lined alleys. Twirl around in the streets when it starts to rain, and nestle yourself by the fire when the weather gets cold. Embrace every texture of this journey, for it is all beautiful in its own way.

It's been an honor to guide you through this book, and I want you to know that if you need further support, it doesn't have to end here. Head over to www.CassandraBodzak.com/Eatwithlntention for many free resources (meditations, cooking videos, and advice) to enrich your own journey to eat with intention.

I'm also delighted to invite you to our thriving "mind-body-soul" support community, www.aprecity.com. I run intensive online workshops twice a month that overflow with meditations and mindful recipe content. Aprecity also has a community forum where you can ask questions, share stories, and connect with others. It allows me to hold the space for you to create the life that LIGHTS you up and keep you on track when life feels out of control. I hope you will join us over there and utilize this powerful tool to integrate all the positive shifts you've made.

Say hi to me on social media at @CassandraBodzak. I would LOVE to hear from you and see your food photos and your #Eatwithlntention book #shelfies. Show me where you are bringing this book, what meditations you love, and what really hit home for you along your journey. I'll say hi right back and share it with the rest of our amazing community!

May you always Eat with Intention
and
Live a life that LIGHTS you up,

Cassandra